CONFIDENCE TRICKS –PRESENTER-

by

ALAN MARS

ISBN 978-1-291-29883-3

First Edition

To Harriet,
with love.

Alan Mars

'The feedback we have received from the attendees has been extremely positive, and I am sure that your coaching helped us to deliver our presentations with greater confidence and skill.'
Ian Burrell, Manufacturing Director, Cadbury Trebor Bassett

'Alan has had a profound impact on my public speaking skills. His calm and methodical approach has really helped me grow and strengthen in the public speaking arena. He's an outstanding coach with brilliant attention to detail.'
Anwar Harland-Khan, CEO at Sustain Worldwide

'We used Alan as a voice coach on several of our NLP programmes over the years. He is unique - fun, inventive, knowledgeable and positive. Our delegates always gave excellent feedback on his work.'
Ian Newton, Stenhouse Consulting

'Alan Mars has presented several workshops for the Society of Teachers of the Alexander Technique CPD Programme. Alan has detailed knowledge of his subject and his workshops are relaxed and friendly. All participants receive confidence and encouragement from him … an interesting subject.'
Stephanie Smith, at Posture PitStop

'Alan Mars is a highly competent voice coach, who has a quite remarkable ability to engage with a very diverse range of people, lead them through the landscape of their personal learning barriers & into an area where their acceptance & confidence in themselves & others is transformed. He is a joy to work with.'
Brian De Lord, Owner Pupil Parent Partnership Ltd.

'I am a trainer and I deliver courses on presentation skills. This book is now my 'give away' instead of my own manual. It says everything I want to say...but better. Frankly, people are more likely to read it…'
H. Ward, Amazon review for 'Presenter'

PREFACE

My first book, 'Presenter – Be Your Best… and Beyond' *(Hodder Arnold, 2003)*, is a guide to motivating teams and individuals to improving their key skills in presenting. This book sets to greatly expand on that text, with the addition of the latest examples and practices that can help the individual further achieve their aim – confidence, style and success.

People are increasingly looking for ways of preserving and building equanimity and poise at work, play and in relationships in general. This is especially true with the financial situation in the world at the moment.

There has been explosion of interest in matters postural, so I have expanded the chapter on postural landmarks considerably. An appendix has been added on the Alexander Technique constructive rest position – simple, rewarding and inexpensive!

The techniques in this book extend beyond the world of public speaking. When I was in New York several years ago, I was looking for books on golf and failed to find them in the sports section. I was surprised to eventually find the golf books in the business section. It doesn't seem to be the same in the UK and Ireland – golf really does seem to be a, serious, leisure pursuit. A lot of the positive feedback I've had has been from golfers.

Like many other presentation skills trainers, I loved to quote the Merhabian statistics -the so called fact that up to 93% of the impact of your presentation is non-verbal with the words accounting for as little as 7% of your total impact. I myself have been guilty of propagating this particular myth. Even Dr Mehrabian, who conducted the original studies, has stated that they were never meant to be applied to normal conversation and certainly not public speaking.

However, I do believe that improving posture, body language and vocal delivery can add tremendously to the power of communication and make the words - the message - much more accessible to an audience.

There are many examples, such as Luciano Pavarotti who had mass appeal and whose handkerchief was uniquely identifiable, becoming inextricably linked to his performances of rousing operatic arias, international football events, the Three Tenors etc… so Pav is still in.

Bill Clinton is now out of the public eye but the examples of creative repetition in his speech (in Chapter 6, Page 104) still hold good – so Bill is still in the book.

I'm happy to say that I haven't owned a television for many years. My impression is that the television audiences have largely fragmented with the increasing number of ways to access news and entertainment. Apart from some so-called reality TV programmes, television as a collective experience seems to have fizzled out.

I used quite a few examples from the banking and mortgage industry in the first edition. Given the events of the past few years – massive recession linked with widespread banking failure - some examples are still in and some are comprehensively out.

Acknowledgements

To be a coach is to spend your life constantly learning from others. One learns most from those to whom one is closest, so the biggest "Thank you" to beloved family – Morwenna, Camilla, Clara, Steve, Douglas, Phyllis, Jennifer, Rudi and Ben!

Heartfelt thanks to dear friends and their lifelines of support over the years – I couldn't have done it without you.

Deep appreciation to the few eagle eyed and perceptive readers who have corrected my shambolic writing – you know who you are!

Three fine women for specific mention – Clara Miriam for her lovely drawings, Kiersty Boon for her painstaking editing skills and Cheryl Winter for contributing sections to the book. Also, Miranda Fairbarn for her semi-supine illustrations.

And finally, thanks to all the people who have attended individual coaching and group courses over the last three decades – you have enriched my life immeasurably.

TABLE OF CONTENTS

- CHAPTER FOUR -

- CHAPTER SEVEN -

- CHAPTER EIGHT -

- CHAPTER NINE -

- CHAPTER TEN -

INTRODUCTION

THESE SHOES WERE MADE FOR TALKIN'

The late Dirk Bogarde found that when he got the right pair of shoes that fitted the personality of the character he was playing, everything else fell into place.

Surely there is more to performing than finding the right pair of shoes? Yes, of course there is, but for Dirk Bogarde the totality of his acting experience somehow became anchored to the shoes.

The information and exercises in this book come from my own thirty years experience as a presenter and from numerous other sources. I have my own pair of shoes. They are fairly flexible and, as an interim measure, have fitted a lot of people. I invite you to try them and walk in them for a while. However, with increasing practise and experience, I am confident that you will find your own pair of shoes.

UNLIMITED IMPROVEMENT

In Neuro Linguistic Programming (NLP), there is a model of learning that describes the journey from unconscious incompetence through to unconscious competence:

Unconscious Incompetence

Before you embark on learning a new skill you are unconscious of the skill-set required and therefore incompetent in its delivery.

In learning to drive a car you simply do not know which control is which - apart from the steering wheel.

Another scenario is that of someone who believes that they are performing well but then receives feedback from others of areas that need further attention! This scenario commonly precedes the onset of the speaker seeking presentation skills coaching.

Conscious Incompetence

Anyone who has learnt how to drive a manual shift car will remember that stage of knowing what is required of you but being unable to coordinate everything – clutch, accelerator, brake, mirrors, signals, manoeuvres!

Conscious Competence

You can now carry out the whole skill set smoothly and competently but you probably do not want be distracted by conversations with passengers or having the radio playing – you still need to think about it.

Unconscious Competence
All the skills have become smoothly, streamlined and unconscious. This frees up conscious awareness for other tasks – conversing with passengers, re-planning your route, listening to music etc. When required you can respond appropriately and seemingly instinctively to the changing conditions of the road and traffic.
The majority of people seek coaching as a result of their experiences in the areas of Conscious Incompetence and Conscious Competence. Strangely enough the people who are least likely to rest on their laurels are those who exhibit Unconscious Competence. This is true in the areas of art, music, sport and, of course, in performance and presentation. Committed practitioners are famous for their attitude of constantly refining even the most basic skills.

RINGING THE BELL

'...a moment of consciousness, however you achieve it, lasts. It has an effect on ones habitual functioning for much longer than the duration of the moment. Rather like the sound of a bell. You strike a bell and it goes on reverberating long after it has been struck.'
Adam Nott, Senior teacher of the Alexander Technique

Refining a skill doesn't benefit much from frowning concentration and determination. It benefits more from mindfulness and light touch correction. In riding a bicycle for the first time you may fall off to the left. In your desire not to repeat that experience you may over compensate and fall to the right. Before you know it you are riding in style... You are still falling to the left and right very subtly but you have gained in balance, confidence and, with a light touch, transformed falling into constructive forward motion.

- Chapter One -

WHAT IF I WERE A BETTER PRESENTER?

'All the worlds a stage, And all the men and women merely players.'
William Shakespeare, 'As You Like It'

'All the worlds a stage and most of us are desperately unrehearsed.'
Sean O'Casey

WHAT WOULD MAKE ME BETTER?

Imagine for a moment what it would be like if you were a better presenter. What would you see in your not-too-distant future? Would you, perhaps, have more of that confidence and composure that is so desirable and so enviable in others? Don't you love it when the skilled performer in any field makes it all look so effortless, so natural? Perhaps you are already a good presenter. But what if you could have those qualities even more reliably, stronger and for longer? How would it affect your confidence and your personal presence? How would it affect you professionally and personally? More job satisfaction? More money? Exciting challenges?

2500 Years of Theatre

The roots of our present theatrical tradition stretch back 2500 years to its origins in classical Greek theatre and oratory. Every time you go to the theatre or cinema, or simply watch adverts on the television, you will be watching actors using techniques drawn from this ancient tradition. Since those times and before, performers have used a wide variety of techniques to propel them into a resourceful state of mind, body and voice from which to give an impactful performance.

The chapters which follow present a number of techniques drawn from the performing arts and a variety of other sources. These techniques are specifically tailored for use in a wide variety of business contexts: presentation and communication skills, coaching skills, leadership training, influencing with integrity and dealing with challenging people and challenging situations.

Anchoring

One of the most important presentation techniques is anchoring. An anchor is a device for stabilizing a sailing vessel, large or small, in a potentially unstable and stormy medium, i.e. the sea. In performance terms, an anchor is a specific stimulus that stabilizes certain conditions of body and mind in the potentially unstable and stormy medium called life. This is often done unconsciously in the form of various lucky charms.

Case Study - Luciano Pavarotti

When Luciano Pavarotti sang in public he would use certain 'tricks' that made him feel more secure.

Pavarotti spoke about his use of a handkerchief on stage:

'Everybody knows about my white handkerchief, which I used in my first concert in Missouri in 1973, in case I started to perspire. I find that I feel much better if I have it out there with me. It has a function but it's also for good luck'.

If you are too young to remember Luciano Pavarotti, do a YouTube search to get a sense of his larger than life presence.

Case Study - Jack Welch, chief executive of General Electric from 1981—2001

Jack Welch had a briefcase nicknamed 'Mr Lucky' by his personal assistant. He won Mr Lucky at a golf tournament in 1977 and, despite looking decrepit, it went with him everywhere...

'I've done extremely well with Mr Lucky. It's been good to me and I never wanted to give it up.'

So how is it possible to take these external lucky charms and internalize them? How can a lucky charm transform from haphazard luck to a regular, reliable resource?

THE WISDOM OF INSECURITY

Performing artists can help you with confidence and with vocal and physical presence, but that is where any similarity between business and theatre work ends... isn't it? Actually, the similarities between mainstream business and the performing arts are increasing all the time. Until about 25 years ago a skilled and conscientious worker could reasonably expect to spend decades, if not their whole working life, in a given job. Nowadays, short-term contracts are increasingly popular. To spend as much as ten years in one company is now the exception rather than the rule.

The world of the performing arts, on the other hand, has always been insecure. The majority of skilled and talented artists live a rather precarious financial existence. Successful performance artists become adept at consciously developing a sense of inner security and confidence that persists regardless of external circumstances. Or, as the veteran British comedian Bob Monkhouse puts it:

'And the moral is: if you're a superstitious person and derive comfort from some lucky mascot, keep it with you — don't depend on it so much that its loss will weaken your self assurance. There's only one charm you should rely on - your own.'

If you want a lifetime of employability and more, then make sure that your lucky charm lives with you, in your centre, at all time. To find out how, read on…

TOOLS FOR YOUR JOURNEY

When eating a cake, some ingredients are virtually invisible to the naked tongue. The egg is one example of this. The fruit, nuts, icing or cherry on top may be the ingredients that make your mouth water, but you would certainly notice if the egg was not there as the whole cake would run the risk of falling apart. The egg does a fantastic job of blending diverse ingredients together into a palatable, delicious whole. Amongst the whole variety of tantalizingly different cakes, certain ingredients crop up again and again.

There are no new ingredients in this book but there are some new combinations of ingredients (theories and practical exercises) and some unique flavours (the voices of those who have achieved great things) to inspire and motivate you.

Eyes and Ears

For people leading busy lives, there is so much going on that it seems necessary to screen out most distractions just to get from A to B. The next time you are travelling during rush hour, pause for a moment and wake up. Look around you. How many other people are truly awake? How many are frowning and chewing over thoughts unrelated to the present moment? How many have a good awareness of what is going on all around them? And how many have tunnel vision? The ability to chew over past and future, and to narrow down attention on to specific goals, is a great blessing and uniquely human. But it can also be a curse...

Terry Pratchett, a best-selling British author, can always be relied upon for a fresh and humorous take on most subjects. Take the popular idea that we only use a fraction of our total brain. Wrong. According to Mr Pratchett all of the brain is used to very efficiently dampen reality. The brain can turn the wonders of life into the mundane and humdrum. Why? He surmised that if this wasn't the case then people...

'faced with the wondrousness of everything, would go around wearing big stupid grins... Part of the brain exists to stop this happening. It is very efficient. It can make people experience boredom in the middle of marvels.'

Wake up and use your eyes and ears. The world is full of the most marvellous examples of communication and presentation skills. And if you don't already have them yourself... steal them! The wonderful thing about behavioural theft is that you can enrich yourself without impoverishing anyone else.

GETTING STARTED

How do you approach a book? Are you a skimmer, a dipper, a beginning to ender? Do you prefer information or practical exercises? Do you go for text or graphics? All these learning styles, or any mixture of them, can be accommodated within this book.

You, the amateur or professional, a new or experienced communicator, will learn how to get into an optimum physical and mental state for making your presentation. Human beings are intrinsically gregarious creatures and, given the best contexts for development, they grow into naturally excellent communicators. However, not all of us have been graced with the best contexts for development. This is where the value of the exercises comes in.

Many of the exercises in this book are subtractive. They involve a process of letting go of the habits that hinder easy expression. Other exercises are additive. They plant a seed that grows and develops over the course of time.

Terminology

The book uses the word 'presenter' and it is used throughout in a general way. It relates to those in business environments, education, community and all those involved in the business of communication, whether it be small, large, formal or informal groups. The words 'audience' or 'listeners' refer to classes, trainees, teams, clients etc.

Working with the exercises

Some people will prefer to work through each exercise in sequence, while others will prefer to read the whole book first in order to become familiar with the thinking behind it. Either approach is legitimate. Some sections of the book may seem more appropriate to your needs than others. You may wish to focus on a select few exercises for some time before moving on. Keeping a journal in which you note down brief details of how the work is progressing can be very helpful. Loosen tight or uncomfortable clothing so that you can breathe and move more freely. A real luxury would be to work with a friend or colleague and to guide each other through an exercise. It is also possible to read an entire exercise a few times, silently or aloud, and then refer to the instructions periodically as you go along. Take enough time to approach the exercises in a calm and unhurried way. If you have only ten minutes to spare, try working with a smaller chunk of a longer exercise. If you have any degree of physical disability, you can easily adapt all the exercises to suit your particular situation.

Materials

A hand-held digital recorder is an inexpensive and portable way of getting unbiased feedback about your presentations. You will also need one or two full-length mirrors in which to observe yourself while carrying out some of the exercises.

A positive attitude

Remember that seriousness, grim determination and striving for results are counter-productive. The qualities that will enhance your work and speed up your progress are:

- humour
- curiosity
- patience
- a playful attitude.

The changes that you make in any one session will usually be fairly small but if you work in an easy and consistent way you will be surprised at how quickly they accumulate. A little goes a long way.

If you find that your attention and actions are parting company during the exercises, pause for a moment or two and gently let them come back together again. If your mind keeps wandering, stop the exercise and come back to it later. Two minutes of easy work is better than an hour of frowning concentration. Enjoyment is the key to continuing motivation.

- Chapter Two -

WHAT DOES BETTER LOOK LIKE?

'Presence: The quality of self-assurance and effectiveness that permits a performer to achieve a rapport with the audience: stage presence.'
American Heritage Dictionary of the English Language

STYLE

There is enormous scope for personal style in the world of presentation. It is fantastic when you get things right by instinct but it can be an unreliable ally. Fortunately, training and application substitute extremely well for instinct. With sufficient repetition, some aspects of training become extremely efficient and streamlined. They turn into an unconscious competence - a learned instinct. This frees up your conscious awareness for other things, enhancing your flexibility and fluidity as a presenter.

Practical Exercise

As a first step towards unconscious competence, you need to identify some of the answers to these questions:

- What does a compelling presenter look like?
- What do they sound like?
- How do they make you feel?

The responses often take the following form: 'A compelling presenter is confident, assured, has authority, relates to the audience, etc.'

But confident, assured and authoritative may mean something slightly different to each person. Now use your eyes and ears to answer these questions:

- How does confidence stand?
- How does confidence walk?
- How does confidence look the audience in the eye?
- At what pace and pitch does confidence speak?

The singer and the song

Robin Prior, co-author of NLP and the 'New Bazaar, A Guide to Sales Training', says that there are two aspects to any presentation: the song and the singer, i.e. what you say and how you say it. The 'what' consists of the words and language. The 'how' consists of body language and the voice.

This 'how' factor is composed largely of the presenter's visual impact - posture, movement, gesture - and their voice - tone, pitch, flexibility and volume.

Even acknowledged experts lose their audience's attention through poor vocal and physical presentation. A nervous, jarring delivery or a boring, monotonous tone, accompanied by a matching style of body

language will rapidly communicate the discomfort of the speaker to the audience.
When the body language and voice quality is sufficiently compelling, it draws the audience toward the 'song', i.e. the message that the presenter is endeavouring to convey.

Alive relaxation
Other speakers have the enviable ability to maintain a state of alive relaxation during their presentations. This is communicated to the audience by the way in which the speaker stands and moves, and through the flexibility and tone of their voice. This increases the audience's attention level and ensures that the presenter manages to get the message across.
All of these qualities can seem frustratingly out of reach for many people. But developing this quality of alive relaxation is not as difficult as it appears. A good start to changing this state of affairs is to develop a much clearer idea of what alive relaxation in presentation looks like, sounds like and feels like.

Practical Exercise - Observe
Observe family, friends and colleagues as they interact. When do they peak? What happens physically and vocally?

VITAL INGREDIENTS FOR THE COMMUNICATION CAKE

What a delicious cake! But what are the ingredients? How is it made? There are three piles of ingredients - the visual, the vocal and the verbal. Each is full of a tantalizing variety of delicious ingredients:

Visual - Presenter's body language:

- Stature
- Head-neck-shoulder relationship
- Facial expression
- Eye contact
- Gestures
- Stillness/movement
- Owning space
- Proximity

Auditory - Presenter's voice:

- Volume/resonance
- Pace, rhythm and articulation
- Pitch and variation
- Silence and pause

Verbal - Presenter's language:

- Structure and sequence
- Accessibility - clear English etc.
- Engagement - stories, metaphors, analogies
- Individuality - sensory words

By managing the physical, vocal and verbal aspects of your presentation skilfully, a door will be opened. This door gives your audience access to your words and to the message that they convey. This door is called 'rapport'.

OBSERVATION AND FEEDBACK

One of the benefits of attending a course on presentation skills is to get skilful support and feedback from the course facilitator. Feedback from other members of the group can also be very useful if it is done constructively. In the absence of a presentation skills course you can use television, radio and, finally, real life to assess what you find compelling, or otherwise, in the way that people communicate. Start by focusing on the visual. Then move on to the vocal. And finally move onto the verbal.

Visual

Watch a television programme with the sound turned down. Make notes about the presenter or actor's body language:

- Posture
- Head-neck-shoulder relationship
- Facial expression
- Eye contact
- Gestures
- Stillness/movement
- Owning space
- Proximity to others

Turn to programmes you wouldn't normally watch - the body language may well be quite different.

If you are feeling adventurous, copy some of the body language. If you can copy it, you are almost certainly seeing it clearly.

Vocal

Listen to the television with the sound on and your eyes closed. Try copying how the presenter is speaking. Don't worry if you don't actually sound like the person you are copying. The purpose of the copying is to make you listen to the voice of the presenter or actor. Now make notes on their voice:

- Volume
- Pace and rhythm
- Articulation
- Pitch and variation
- Resonance
- Silence and pause

Every now and then open your eyes and check to see how much the voice and the body language match or mismatch each other.
Listen to the radio, especially talk-intensive programmes. Is there a difference between radio and television delivery?

Verbal
Finally, bring the words into the equation by analysing them in this way:

- Accessibility — simple, clear language
- Structure and sequence of the subject
- Use of stories, metaphors and analogies

Sensory words:

- visual, auditory and feeling words
- words describing taste and smell

Can you think of a presenter who has a good balance of all three?
Keep your eyes and ears open. Enjoy the variety and richness around you.

WHO ARE YOUR FAVOURITE PRESENTERS?

There are an absolute host of them out there. Excellent role models come from every walk of life - work, community, media, theatre, politics, friends and family. What do they do that grabs your attention? Do these role models engage other people's attention to the same degree that they engage yours? Just how common is it to find an excellent model of communication and presentation skills?

Many people are in the position of having to deliver set presentations. While this may be restricting from one point of view, from another it can be quite liberating. As long as the set presentation is of a sufficiently good quality, and in line with your beliefs and values, it can be a platform from which to explore the more performance-related, non-verbal aspects of presentation. After all, most actors and singers spend the majority of their performing career using other people's words, mostly to very good effect.

Practical Exercise - Your own radio report

So, who is your favourite presenter? In this exercise you will become a radio reporter who is bringing their favourite presenter to life in the minds of their listeners. Speaking into a tape/ digital recorder is not essential but it helps many people to get into character. Remember, this is not live radio. It doesn't have to be perfect. It can be edited a later stage or you can have several attempts until you feel satisfied.

1. Think of someone who is a good presenter. They can be from as broad a category as you like — work, television, theatre, social or family. It could refer to formal or informal presentations.
2. When you are with this person, what do you see? Describe this out loud into your recorder. Paint as vivid a word picture as possible. Remember that it is going to be broadcast to radio listeners nationwide.
3. Start with the most basic information first — the name of your presenter and your relationship to them. For example:

   Hello. I would like to introduce you to my favourite presenter. His/her name is __________ and he/she is (my boss, cousin, colleague, a well-known star of stage and screen...)
4. Now describe your presenter in the most basic terms — height, age, gender, how they dress, etc.:

   Janet/John is about __________ tall.

5. How do they sit, stand or move when they are speaking. What is their eye contact like?
   Janet/John moves about quite a lot while presenting and every now and then when he/she really wants to make an important point he/she stands very still and holds your gaze for a long time...
6. What do you hear? How do they speak — fast/slow; high/low?
   She/he speaks quietly but audibly with lots of variation...
7. What kind of language or speech do they use?
   Janet speaks very simply and to the point, without being patronizing; John is a real storyteller; often going off at tangents and bringing the strands together at the end...
8. Having brought your presenter to life in the minds of your listeners go on to tell them a bit more about why you find the presenter so compelling. If some of their magic could rub off onto you, what would it be?
9. Conclude your presentation:
   And that was my favourite presenter; Janet/John Smith. Thank you and goodbye from me, your roving reporter — . Tune in again next week for the next exciting episode.

Case Study - Maria

Maria works for a large financial institution. She was eager to forward her career as much as possible over the next few years. She came to me for training because she had a tendency to race ahead in her speech. She wanted to become calmer and more authoritative through pacing her speech more effectively.

To help Maria do this, we worked on a Shakespeare sonnet that not only helped her to slow down her speech but also to speak with a fuller and more resonant quality.

Sonnet 18

Shall I compare thee to a summer's day?
Thou art more lovely and more temperate:
Rough winds do shake the darling buds of May,
And summer's lease hath all too short a date:
Sometime too hot the eye of heaven shines,
And often is his gold complexion dimm'd;
And every fair from fair sometime declines,
By chance or nature's changing course untrimm'd;
But thy eternal summer shall not fade
Nor lose possession of that fair thou owest;
Nor shall Death brag thou wander'st in his shade,
When in eternal lines to time thou growest:
So long as men can breathe or eyes can see,
So long lives this and this gives life to thee.

We recorded each recitation, then moved on to some exercises. After this we would go through the process of reciting, recording and listening again. Maria's use of her voice gradually improved with each successive repetition. The radio reporter exercise (described above) brought together all the previous strands that we had been working on. When Maria started to describe her favourite presenter, she began to use strong, powerful gestures and a more measured, confident voice. She eliminated the hesitant gestures that can often be seen as the visual equivalent of tripping over or struggling to find the right words.
Maria recited her sonnet once again. It had improved considerably. Some of the qualities that she found so appealing in her chosen presenter had spontaneously been incorporated into her body language and voice. Please go Chapter 14, The Practised Pause, to find out more.

Practical Exercise – Mind's Eye, Mind's Ears

This is an exercise you can try anywhere. It utilises your mind's eye, your mind's ears and your immediate responses. But be careful — if you do this in a public place some of the results could make you laugh out loud and could attract some alarmed or concerned glances from those around you!

1. Take a moment to think about your body. Get as close as possible to a pleasantly neutral physical and mental place. Let go of any unnecessary tension. Make sure your weight is evenly distributed between your left and right feet if you are standing and between your left and right buttocks if you are sitting.
2. Now use your mind's ear to conjure up a voice with the quality of nails dragging down a blackboard — a grating sound. Having noticed your physical and other responses to that voice, return to your pleasantly neutral state.
3. Repeat the same procedure for a number of other voices:
   - boring
   - authoritative
   - clear but fairly neutral
   - passionate and engaging
   - sexy.
4. You may find that as you get a voice in your mind's ear, an image of a particular person will pop up to accompany it.
5. Repeat this exercise the other way around. Conjure up images in your mind's eye of the qualities listed above then think about the voice.

DELIVERY

For any script, text or presentation, a wide range of deliveries is possible. These range from the uncomfortable (for both speaker and listener) to the compelling and engaging.

You may or may not recall the actor Peter Sellers performing a spoken rendition of the Beatles song 'A Hard Day's Night' dressed in Elizabethan costume. He delivered it in a serious, declamatory, mock-Shakespearean style that had its intended effect — incongruous and comedic. Look it up on youtube where you will find many other examples of comedic incongruity.

In most circumstances you will want to be as congruent as possible when presenting, with body, voice, feeling and message all knitting together. But the very incongruity of comedy can highlight beautifully those qualities that bring engagement and rapport to a presentation.

Practical Exercise – The Grand Old Duke of York

Take some of the voices above —boring, authoritative, clear but fairly neutral, passionate and engaging, sexy. Imagine them reading the nursery rhyme below. Read it out loud in each type of voice.

'Oh, the Grand Old Duke of York,
He had ten thousand men.
He marched them up to the top of the hill
And he marched them down again!
And when they were up they were up
And when they were down they were down.
And when they were only half way up
They were neither up nor down.'

LISTEN AND LEARN

When you next listen to a presentation, analyse the constituent elements that make up that person's voice (you could do the same with their body language). You will soon start to realize why you respond to different speakers in different ways. For example, if a grating voice creates tension in you, it is likely that the speaker is, at that moment at least, also experiencing stress on some level. What about the quiet authority of a particular newsreader's voice? You will also see it reflected in their physical demeanour. In the course of daily life, become more sensitive to the variety of voices around you. Keep your eyes open, too - does a person's body language and voice seem to match or mismatch?

The Home Ham-let

People who have busy professional and home lives often complain that they have no opportunities to practise voice work. In fact, if you have young children you have a wonderful opportunity to practise.

When you read them a story, bring some of your vocal qualities into the voices of the different characters. Ham it up! Exaggerate! Ninety-nine times out of a hundred they will absolutely love it… and love you. And that is exactly what most presentations are about… winning the love of the really important few.

If you don't have children to practise with, recite some nursery rhymes or children's stories to a willing listener who has a high tolerance for eccentric behaviour.

Case Study – Interview with Robin Prior

Robin Prior is a writer and performance skills trainer for business and the arts

RP: "The great presenters are people who are totally 'in' the subject. With some presenters it's like 'I'm the presenter. This is the subject. We are separate. So if you don't like the subject you can still like me.' The compelling presenters are those people who are totally committed to it, totally inside it, don't want to be separated from it. It is almost as if the subject starts in the middle of them, at their centre of gravity and then radiates out, like those ornaments where if you touch the side the electrical force sparks out and comes to meet your finger.

A great example of this commitment is Billy Connolly, because he is 100 per cent present. He takes a risk because he doesn't have a script - he just has some subjects that he works with. And he takes it on trust that he is going to do it and it happens. You never get a sense with Billy Connolly that he is delivering material. He is there with you in a way that a really good presenter never just delivers material.

I think he is a genius at communicating. There are obviously going to be other parts of him that you don't see but you get this sense when you see him that you are getting Billy Connolly and not a stage persona. Total commitment, 100 per cent doing, 100 per cent there, not holding back.

What I get from someone like Billy Connolly is that they are giving me all that they can give me. I find that very respectful. If I am working with a group of people, I'm not there just because they are paying me lots of money. These people have committed time to this so it is only respectful for me to give them everything while I am there. I am committed to their outcomes, for that presentation."

AM: "So there is none of 'I'll hold this back for stage two, for the second course'?"

RP: "There is only so much content you can handle. There is certain amount that people will learn at any given time and it is different for different people. And you have to gauge that by looking at their response rates and attention. But whatever you do with content, you must apply yourself to it 100 per cent."

- Chapter Three -

CREATING A COMPELLING GOAL

'I am the most spontaneous speaker in the world because every word, every gesture and every retort has been carefully rehearsed.'
George Bernard Shaw

'Imagination is the beginning of creation.'
George Bernard Shaw

THROUGH POISE TO PURPOSE

She stands in the middle of the room, gazing through the plate glass window. She is standing in an easily upright manner, weight distributed, head balanced, shoulders easy and wide. She is dressed in smart business attire. Her name is Celia. On closer inspection her eyes are somewhat unfocused. She is, apparently, talking out loud to herself. She is giving a rich verbal description of someone, also called Celia, who is giving an excellent presentation:

'Celia pauses briefly. She is physically and emotionally composing herself, before she enters the room. She's ready now. Celia enters the room and stands at her full height and width. She smiles at the group of people and says, 'Good morning everyone!' in a clear, ringing voice. She's certainly got everybody's attention as she walks up to the podium. She is now taking a moment to calmly sort out her notes. She puts the notes down, looks up and makes warm eye contact with people on the left, on the right and then in the middle of her audience. She is now saying, 'Good morning. My name is Celia Wallace' to the left of the audience; 'I am a manager from Human Resources', while looking to the right of the audience, 'and today I am going to talk to you about our team strategy for next year', as she looks to the middle.'

Should we be alarmed at this unusual behaviour? Seek urgent medical advice?

Celia is practising a technique, beloved of sports psychologists, that gives athletes a leg-up into the peak performance zone. She is talking her performance through from a third person perspective. This detached perspective allows her to imagine herself giving the presentation her best possible shot. It helps her to reduce her habitual feelings of panic at the prospect of giving a presentation.

Many professional sports teams employ sports psychologists who use a variety of techniques to help the team members improve their performance. At the forefront of these techniques are procedures that harness the power of the imagination.

Such techniques were studied by psychologist Alan Richardson. A group of subjects received coaching in how to take free throws at a basketball basket. They were then split into three separate groups. Group One was instructed to practise free throws for 20 minutes per day. Group Two visualized doing free throws for 20 minutes per day. Group Three did no practice at all. The results at the end of twenty days were surprising. The 'real' practice group (Group One) improved by 24 per cent. The visualization group (Group Two) improved by 23 per cent. Group Three, unsurprisingly, did not improve at all.

The imagination has no bar to perfection. There is nothing to stop the least skilled player from imagining themselves engaging in the pinnacle of sporting activity or, in your case, presentational feats of the highest level of skill. While this does not automatically guarantee that you will become a world-class presenter or sports personality, it does provide a way in which you can rise into your peak performance zone.

THE VMBR STUDIES

In another study Dr Richard Suinn, of Colorado State University, developed a method called Visio-Motor Behaviour Rehearsal (VMBR). This combines deep muscle relaxation exercises with mental imaging of the skill that is being learned.

In one study thirty-two new karate students were placed into four groups. Each student underwent an anxiety and skills test, then each group was given a different home practice to do over the following six weeks:

Group 1: Deep muscle relaxation only

Group 2: Imaging only — visualizing the karate techniques in the mind's eye

Group 3: VMBR — relaxation exercises followed by visualization

Group 4: No home practice of any description.

At the end of the six-week period, the students were again given anxiety tests. They were also given a traditional karate grading test. The VMBR and relaxation-only group both recorded lower levels of anxiety than the other groups. In the sparring tests, the VMBR group demonstrated a clear superiority.

The same method that can help a karate practitioner to reduce anxiety and increase skill for the purposes of examination can be used to help you increase your verbal and non-verbal composure and reduce your anxiety at the prospect of presenting.

AN INTRODUCTION TO ALIVE RELAXATION

The karate-based study mentioned in the last section says it all - most presenters want to be able to reduce their anxiety and improve their performance.

'Personal presence' depends on the practice of surprisingly simple yet fundamental skills. The exercises that follow are similar to those that an actor would use to prepare voice and body for going on stage.

In this section, you will be exploring the physiology of confidence by visiting a number of physical landmarks on your own body:

- Your centre of gravity
- Your feet and how your body weight drops through them into the ground.

In the following sections, we will also explore the power and impact of balancing your head freely on top of your spine.

Having familiarized yourself with these physical landmarks of confidence you will find it very easy to practise them. Waiting in line - in shops, at traffic lights, for tickets - instead of getting bored or frustrated, you will now be able to practise and reinforce your new strategies.

YOUR CENTRE OF GRAVITY

In 1681, Neapolitan mathematician, Giovanni Borelli, made novel use of a see-saw to determine the centre of gravity of the human body. He laid a person down flat across a see-saw. The see-saw would become evenly balanced only when the person had their full weight equally distributed on either side of the pivot. Borelli determined from this that the centre of gravity was located between the buttocks and the pubic bone, just in front of the sacrum — the wide, wedge-shaped bone that comprises the base of the spine.

This principle applies when standing, too. When you are balanced the weight of your whole body is evenly distributed from left to right, from front to back, from the very top of the head, through the centre of gravity and all the way down to the soles of your feet. The shoulders sit easily on either side of this gravity line. The statues from the archaic period of ancient Greece are like this — beautifully poised, upright and balanced and consequently require very small plinths to prevent them toppling.

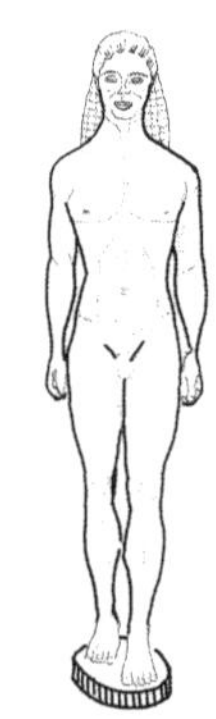

Figure A

Figure B

Statues of the later periods, Greek and Roman, are more asymmetrical and unbalanced from front to back. They require huge plinths and other props, such as tree stumps, to stop them from falling over.

Human beings do not have plinths; we rely on muscular tension to stop us from falling over when we are out of balance. We have to take responsibility for our own co-ordination and balance. Being psychologically balanced and centred is intimately related to being physically balanced and centred.

The gravity line drops from the head, through the centre and between the two feet as shown Figure A. In the Figure B, the line drops from the top of the head through the centre, through the front of the knee and through the middle of the feet. In both cases the body weight is distributed more or less equally to either side of this line.

The Gravity Line

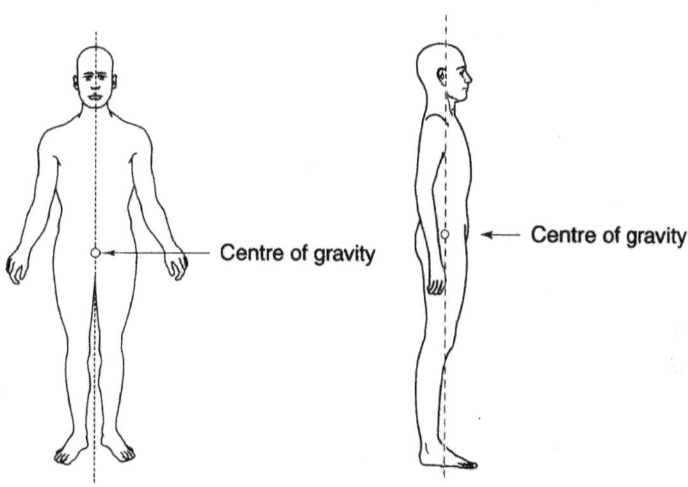

Practical Exercise - Centring

If possible, do the following exercise while standing.

1. If you are standing make sure that your body weight is reasonably well balanced between your left and right feet.
   If you are sitting, distribute your weight evenly between left and right buttocks. Place your feet flat on the floor with the weight evenly distributed – as in standing.
2. Find your own centre of gravity by placing one hand halfway between your navel and your pubic bone. Place your other hand over the corresponding area of your back. The area between your two hands corresponds to your centre of gravity. Pat this section of your body two or three times with your hands, then place your hands back the side.
3. Now turn your attention to what is going on around you. Use your eyes to notice three things - familiar or unfamiliar. And now listen - identify three different sounds.
4. Gently switch between concentrating on your centre of gravity and paying attention to your surroundings, while breathing gently through your nose.

5. Say "Keep centre of gravity", Imagine that your voice is emanating from this centre. Repeat the same phrase internally in your mind's ear.

Practise this centring exercise regularly. Whenever you feel the need to become more centred, place your hands over your centre and repeat the phrase 'Keep centre of gravity' to yourself. This will help you to reach a centred state.

Centring will give you an effective way to control your feelings of fear at the prospect of presenting. Muscle mass accounts for 35-45 per cent of the total weight of your body. Every cell in your brain connects directly or indirectly to muscle. Centring creatively influences this mind-body system, allowing you transform anxiety into excitement.

Case Study - Robert

Robert is head of information technology for an international company. He gives regular presentations. Twice a year he speaks to audiences in excess of five hundred people. In the past this made him extremely apprehensive. Centring has changed all of that for him:

'I find that not only does the work with centring make me feel calmer, it also helps take my mind away from the negative internal dialogue, 'I hope I don't forget my words. I feel faint. I hope I'm not going to keel over,' and so on. Usually just being aware of my centre is sufficient to calm me and keep me on track. Sometimes I just repeat the phrase "Keep centre of gravity" internally. I imagine that my voice is actually emanating from my centre and radiating out to the edges of my body and beyond. This submerges the negative inner voices and allows me to focus more on my presentation and the audience.'

BALANCE AND GROUNDING

Our feet are structured like tripods consisting of the heel and the inner and outer balancing pads, or balls, of each foot. When you stand in a balanced way, your body weight is equally distributed between the left and right feet. Approximately half of your total body weight drops through the heels. The remaining half is distributed between the inner and outer balancing pads. This distribution is not static, of course. There will always be some slight oscillation and adjustment in even the most quietly balanced standing.

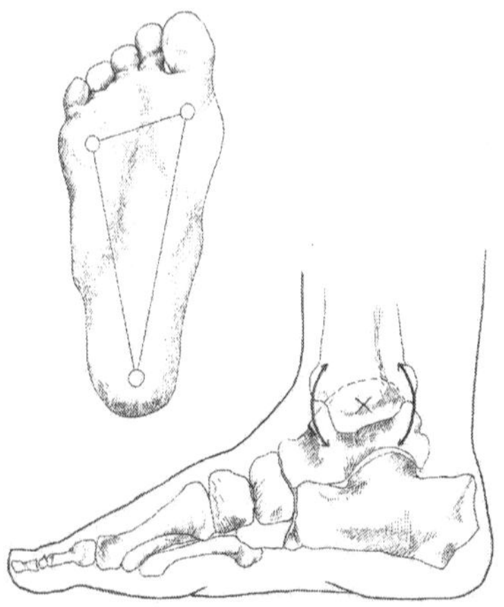

Pictures of ankle and balance tripods

Have you ever noticed people who are physically off balance when they are presenting? Leaning their weight habitually on one leg? Leaning too far forwards or backwards? Legs too far apart, too close together or crossed? More importantly, keep an eye out for the presenters who naturally seem to have a balanced quality. They will almost certainly have a more confident and easy presence.

What upsets your balance?

Have you ever noticed that the sole of one shoe wears out more quickly than the other or that the heels wear quicker than the toes? This is usually the result of habitual weight distribution, for example leaning on a particular leg when standing. You may also notice this favouritism if you cross your legs when sitting.

And why is it that a bag, even a light one, hangs so well off one shoulder but so badly off the other? This could be because that particular shoulder hitches up habitually to provide a nice hook shape. You might be paying a price, in muscular tension, for your handy hook. The heavier the bag is, the more your whole body will compensate by either leaning toward the bag or away from it. This compensation continues to a lesser degree after you put the bag down. Analyse your weight distribution and day-to-day movements and try to remedy anything that throws you off balance. If you carry a bag, put it down whenever you can — let the train, bus or ground take its weight, rather than your shoulder.

Stop, analyse and correct your movements and posture for a few minutes, throughout each day. This will help you to become more grounded and centred, and will allow many muscles to release unnecessary tension.

In the appendix we will explore the Alexander Technique semi-supine resting position which is a fantastically simple and effective way of re-establishing conditions of balance.

Practical Exercise - Footprints in the sand

1. Imagine that you are standing with bare feet on warm, slightly damp sand. Imagine the shape of your footprint in the sand — the roundness of the heels, the outside edge of each foot as it runs up to the little toe, the balls of the feet and the toes. There is virtually no indentation from the inside of the foot where the arch is.
2. You are going to leave two perfect footprints in the sand by ensuring that your body weight is well distributed. Do this by gently swaying your weight from left to right and then from front to back with small subtle movements.
3. As you continue making these left/right and front/back adjustments allow your knees to be soft and responsive to the movements.
4. Now focus your attention on your centre, then on the world around you.
5. Gently shuffle your attention between your footprints, your centre and the world around you. Build up a sense of the unity of these interconnected parts.

Case Study - John

John, who suffered from extreme nerves at the start of every presentation, positively enjoyed giving presentations after the first few awful minutes were over. He knew his job inside out, he produced relaxed, well-written material and was naturally sociable. His audiences always enjoyed his presentations. The first few minutes were the only grit in the machine for him. What would it be like if he could transform that?

'If I could manage the first few minutes more easily, I would do more presentations. Doing more presentations would make me a lot more visible within the company. I think 1 could realistically be up for a senior management position within a few years. I would really like to become a keynote speaker within business circles.'

As John started to work on his centring techniques, he found that getting his weight well distributed over his feet was an immensely useful resource. The anxiety evaporated but would come back again very quickly if he leant with too much weight on his left foot. This was almost certainly connected to a desire to rapidly 'exit stage left'. John put a large paperclip in his left shoe. It was very uncomfortable only if he leant on it. When he stood with his weight distributed it was noticeable, but only barely so. As his body began to adapt, John's confidence increased and he is now presenting better than ever.

PERIPHERAL VISION AND PERSONAL SPACE

Stress - the fight/flight response - is notorious for affecting the way in which we use the eyes. The pupils dilate, heightening visual acuity and, in many cases, leading to a tunnelling of the vision. Coupled with tension in the neck and shoulders, this can lead to the presenter locking on to certain members of the audience, perceived friends or foes, and consequently leaving the rest of the audience feeling somewhat neglected. Taking responsibility for how you use your eyes not only has a calming influence but it also positively influences the way in which audience sees you.

More confident, experienced presenters have an ability to encompass the whole audience with one broad, spacious sweep of their eyes. They can also make soft and personal eye contact with individual members of the audience. The first quality, the broad visual sweep, helps to bring the presenter to his or her full stature and enhances the impression of a larger than life presence. The second quality lends the presenter a feeling of approachability with all its associated qualities.

Peripheral vision

1. Start by remembering your centre and your footprints. Allow your arms to rest at your sides.
2. Link the fingertips of your left and right hands in front of your centre — thumb to thumb, index to index. Smoothly raise your linked fingers until they come to rest, at arm's length, in front of your face.
3. Continue looking straight ahead and move your hands out to your sides until they just start to disappear from the edges of your vision. Move your hands in and out of the edges of your vision a few times.
4. Bring your hands to rest so that they are slightly inside your field of peripheral vision. Your arms will be almost fully extended, as if you were preparing to give someone a big hug. Be aware of the big hemisphere of your vision in front, to the left and right, above and below.
5. Maintain this sense of your hemisphere of vision as you gently bring your arms down to rest at your sides. Be aware of just how much you can see in your peripheral vision.

Peripheral vision seems to be much more closely connected to our sense of movement and orientation in space than focused vision does in isolation.

Practical Exercise - Walking with an expanded visual field
Look at an object at the other end of the room. Walk toward this object and allow your peripheral vision to remain open. As you walk, you may feel as if the walls, floor and ceiling are moving behind you at an equal speed to your movement.
You can expand your visual field at other times — while walking along a road, a corridor, a beach or a country path, for example. Performing artists of all kinds often seem to have a larger than life presence when they are on stage. Expanding your visual field in this way can help you expand your sense of personal space, which is an important stepping stone towards developing presence.

Practical Exercise - Personal space
Extend your arms out to your sides, then turn in a circle and get a sense of fully occupying the space that you are in. Imagine that you are occupying a sphere of personal space —in a circle, below you, above you and all around you. No matter how large it may be, you can brush the boundaries of this space with your fingertips. Bring your hands down to your sides and continue being aware of your centre, roots, expanded vision and personal space.
Your centre is like a tiny seed from which your presence extends in all directions. Excellent presenters have the ability to adjust the size of their personal presence, as appropriate, for different contexts and situations.
A good 'home base' for personal space or presence is one that is at arms' length all around you. Practise this with your peripheral vision and arms gently extended in the privacy of your home, in different-sized rooms. Remember to come back to home base, arms' length around you each time.

Practical Exercise - Walk of Shame or Walk of Fame?

'When you sit, just sit. When you walk, just walk. Above all don't wobble.' Zen Buddhist saying

Performance begins before you stand on the stage. And performances end after you have left the stage.
All eyes tend to be on the performer as they make their way to the stage. In addition to practising your centring, also practice externalising your attention – expanded visual field and personal space – as you approach the stage.
In many situations, you, the performer, may already be in a sitting position when you are called upon to do your turn. Sit like the statue of the Pharaoh and Queen – centred, serene and dignified. Practice making the transition from sitting to standing as smoothly and gracefully as possible.
After having delivered a superb performance some presenters mar the effect by scurrying off the stage – the flight aspect of the fight/flight syndrome. Walk off with as much sparkle, or more, as you walked on with.

Case Study - John Bourke and his All Ireland golf medal
"Ten years ago I set my heart on winning an All-Ireland golf medal. I was playing to a handicap of about 11. With professional golf lessons to improve my swing my handicap dropped to 9.
The mental side of my game needed work and so I bought the golf psychology books by Dr. Bob Rotella and others. I reduced my handicap further to a somewhat insecure 7. The area that did not develop was my control of 'state' i.e. that seemingly elusive combination of mood, physical coordination and mental focus. If I got nervous it affected my performance.
This is where NLP and Alan Mars entered the equation. Alan teaches a combination of Alexander Technique, voice-work, centring and confidence building exercises drawn from the Japanese martial art Aikido and, of course, NLP. He also coached me on how to kill negative self talk by singing while I played.
I took these processes to heart and transferred their application to playing golf. I now felt that I had all the components for excellent

performance i.e. the swing, the routines and a system for maintaining state even in pressurised situations...

'I stand in a bunker 120 yards from the flag. My opponent has just played a shot onto the green and is sitting pretty. The crowd applaud his shot and I know his ball is close to the hole. My caddy advises me to be careful, 'Make sure you clear the lip of the bunker. If you don't, we're in trouble'.

It's a beautiful autumn day, like one of those Indian summers we remember as kids. I listen to the wind rustling in the trees. The birds are chirping away happily. My partner says anxiously 'Do you think you can carry it all the way to the green? This might be a good time to play smart and lay up'.

I hear these comments but I screen them out. I am in fact singing the words of 'King of the Road' and am focussed on the melody. I feel fine as I notice people walking by, stopping to look at my situation and speaking in hushed voices. I screen their words out.

I step out of the bunker and take a look at the green. I see about 100 people standing behind the green - all looking down at me. I keep singing...

I take a practise swing and it feels good. I step back into the bunker, line myself up, shuffle my feet to get a good stance. I breathe in and let the air out slowly and gaze at a branch, high in a tree, behind the green - exactly on the line I wish to aim along. 'Yes', I say, 'That is my target'. I look back at the ball and let the words of the song drift away on the wind. I swing at the ball and watch it soar over the lip of the bunker, high into the air and directly towards the branch. The ball lands 15 feet past the hole on an up-slope. The ball bounces forward and hesitates, shivers... and roles backwards to about a foot from the hole. The crowd erupt in cheers and applause.

I know that I have just played as good a golf shot, under pressure, as Tiger Woods has ever played. A sense of warmth spreads through my body - like sunshine reaching places that have been dark for a long time.

Our opponents never recovered from that shot but it was their comment afterwards that made all the difference.

'I don't know what you had taken before you went out there today' one of them said, 'Whatever it was it made you look unbeatable. You seemed to occupy all the space on the course and left very little room for us. When you played that bunker shot I knew our destiny was sealed and that we would lose'.

Friends tell me that I walked around the course that day as if I didn't have a worry in the world. That's exactly how I felt - a feeling of intense calm and a belief that everything I had ever done up till that day had been in preparation for this. I was now going to enjoy the moment… and I did."

PERCEPTUAL POSITIONS & PERSONAL RELATIONS

Why do some people naturally have a wide range and depth of understanding of all kinds of people, issues and situations? What allows them to penetrate to the heart of a situation and deal with it with flexibility, grace and elegance? When it comes to mentally rehearsing a presentation, or any performance situation, you can do it from at least three different but complementary points of view:

1. **Your own viewpoint**
2. **The perspective of the audience**
3. **The vantage point of a detached yet kindly observer.**

Each individual has their own unique way of viewing the world, as well as a contribution to make, to any given situation. With each of these unique viewpoints comes an equally special set of limitations.
At any time, each of us is capable of consciously processing approximately seven chunks of information. For example, most people will be able to remember a seven-digit phone number. A nine-digit number will be more difficult. If, however, you divide the nine-digit number into three chunks of three digits each, you will again find the whole number easier to recall.
In law courts, different witnesses give evidence on the same event. Depending on their differing vantage points, they may see and hear different things and correspondingly arrive at quite different conclusions. Each witness has their own unique way of selecting which seven chunks of the situation they will attend to. This multiplicity of information enables the judge, as an observer of the proceedings, to develop a fuller picture of the situation.
Each of us is capable of viewing life events and personal or business relationships from a multiplicity of perspectives. The more perspectives we have, the more chunks of information are available for us to guide our choices and behaviour.

PERCEPTUAL TOOLS

The radio reporter revisited

You may like to use a tape or digital recorder for the perceptual position exercises in the following section. The recorder takes the place of a fascinated listener who hangs on to every word of your mental rehearsal strategy as you broadcast it out loud. Your job is to create, like the radio broadcaster, a vivid a mental picture for the listener. It does not matter whether you see the pictures or not — even if you are not a natural visualiser, you will slowly start to increase your ability through using this method. Just as in real radio programmes, you could do the radio report from different points of view.

A little black book

It is useful to carry a small notebook with you as the VMBR strategy also works with writing. It is not only useful for writing mental rehearsal scripts but also for making notes of moments of valuable creative insight and inspiration.

Mental rehearsal ingredients

Mental rehearsal is all very well, but you may be wondering what to rehearse. Here are a few 'openers' - safe, easy chunks of words and language to get you started.

People who are giving presentations are often encouraged to pause powerfully before launching into their presentation. Many speakers, especially when they feel anxious, find this difficult to do. When muscles are overly tense, a pause of a few seconds can seem like a long time. Your centre of gravity is a useful and creative location in which to place your attention during those critical few seconds.

1. Pause for a few seconds and direct your attention on your centre of gravity before you introduce yourself to an imaginary audience. Recite a piece of poetry, a limerick, a nursery rhyme - anything that amuses you. Pause, and re-centre at the end of each line.
2. Now use a more realistic introduction e.g. "My name is (your name) and I work in (your job title) and today I am going to speak about (your choice of subject)."

First perceptual position: your own viewpoint

In this, the first perceptual position, you stand inside your own skin, look out of your own eyes and have your own habitual thoughts and feelings about the world around you and your relationships within it.

From here you engage fully and vitally with the world around you. It is the place from which your choices and decisions are ultimately implemented.

However, you can become stuck in habitual grooves of thought, feeling and attitude that reduce your ability to deal with the challenges of daily life. Travelling around the other perceptual positions, then returning to and updating the first position, is a great help for getting back on track.

First position language and mental rehearsal are characterized by the first-person pronoun:

*"**I**'m here. **I**'ve planned and prepared my words and visual aids. **I**'ve centred myself, warmed up my voice and practised my moves. **I** am now walking on to the stage. **I** see and hear my audience. **I** am ready to speak."*

Second perceptual position: the audience's viewpoint

This, the second perceptual position, is as if you occupy someone else's body, habitual thoughts and feelings. Look out at the world through their eyes and gain a deeper understanding of their feelings, values, needs and perspectives.

At its most basic level, this means knowing your audience:

- What do they want to get out of your presentation?
- If you haven't met any of your audience before, try doing a bit of research on the group or company that you are speaking to.
- Knowing a little of their current concerns can go a long way.
- Knowing some of the current language or jargon is also helpful if used skilfully and sparingly.

The second perceptual position can be used to identify with a member of the audience and observe yourself from their perspective.

Something that does not seem to work well from the presenter's point of view may work brilliantly from the audience's perspective — and vice versa. Feedback from trusted friends and colleagues helps with this, as does recording your presentations.

At a deeper level, the second position involves putting yourself in the other person's shoes and, for a short period, taking on their personal viewpoint:

- Imagine yourself sitting, observing your presentation from the point of view of an audience member.

- As you go through your presentation, watch and listen to yourself from the perspective of that audience member.

How does it make you feel? What impact does your presentation have on you, the audience member? Would you do anything differently as a result?

The language of the second position is characterized by the **third-person pronoun:**

*"**He/she** is now walking on to the stage. **He/she** is pausing and centring him/herself. **He/she** is looking out to the audience. **He/she** is starting to speak."*

This language can also be 'warmed up' by speaking from the perspective of a friendly audience member:

"Celia is now walking on to the stage. And now she is pausing. Celia is starting to speak."

Once you have done this, come back to the first position:

Now that you have seen your presentation from the point of view of a friendly audience, how would you do things differently?

Given the audience's background and their reasons for listening to you, what parts of the jigsaw could you fill in to complete the picture of your presentation?

Third perceptual position: a detached vantage point

In this, the third perceptual position, you become a detached, wise observer of yourself and your way of relating to others. Your focus of vision is broad. The third position utilizes distance to decrease the emotional enmeshment that many experience in difficult situations and enables you to see where the patterns of your own feelings, values and needs as well as those of others dovetail. It also helps you to perceive where you and they are not meeting — so that you can adjust your behaviour accordingly.

The language of the third position is that of the descriptive observer:

*"**He/she** is walking slowly onto the stage. **He/she** is pausing and centring. **He/she** is looking out confidently to the audience. **He/she** is now speaking clearly."*

The third position can be made warmer and more connected by using the performer's name:

"Celia is walking slowly onto the stage now. Celia is pausing and centring herself. Celia is now starting to speak clearly."

With practise, this warm sense of connection can become the voice of the personal coach who is calling out encouragement from the sidelines whenever it is needed.

Third position has wide enough vision to track the relationship between audience and presenter:

"The audience are talking amongst themselves. Celia is walking out onto stage. She pauses and the audience becomes aware of her presence. Celia starts to speak..."

In 'Why I Write', George Orwell describes a form of inner writing that is uncannily close to the third perceptual position:

From childhood until the age of 25, he would construct stories about himself. When he was younger he would be the hero at the centre of thrilling adventures. As he became older, the story-making became more diary-like and centred around whatever activity he was presently engaged with

For minutes at a time this kind of monologue would be running through his brain:

'He pushed the door open and entered the room. A yellow beam of sunlight, filtering through the muslin curtains, slanted on to the table where a matchbox, half-open, lay beside the inkpot. With his right hand in his pocket, he moved across to the window...' etc., etc.'

Orwell reported that he seemed to be constructing these stories almost against his will. They always had the same meticulous descriptive quality that reflected the styles of the various writers he admired.

DEALING WITH DIFFICULTIES

People find perceptual shifts harder to achieve with individuals whom they consider to be difficult or adversarial. It must be emphasised that understanding the other person's point of view does not necessarily mean agreeing with them. It does, however, make it easier to empathize with them.

In a 1950s experiment on anger, the unwitting volunteers were insulted by one of the experimenters, who then quickly left the room. Unaware that they had been set up, the volunteers became angry. Another experimenter explained that the person who had left the room was having a particularly difficult time in their personal life at the moment. The volunteers calmed down very quickly on hearing this information.

In this example, the volunteers shifted from first position (self), to second position and then into the calmness of third position before returning, calmed down and more compassionate, to first position.

This kind of quick shuffle certainly makes it easier to deal with people or situations that you might normally consider to be difficult.

There is a native American expression that says you should not judge another person until you have walked a month in their moccasins. In other words, no matter how crazy their behaviour might seem from your point of view, it will have an internal logic or coherence from where they are standing. That is to say,

There is a positive intention behind every communication.

Is the above statement true? Not in any absolute sense. Is it useful? Incredibly. Before you go on to your next task of the day, try centring yourself and think about some of the people with whom you will be having minor meetings or interactions. Repeat the above phrase to yourself a few times. This centring will reduce your anxiety and increase your flexibility by taking you quickly and automatically through the three perceptual positions. It will increase your respect for other people's point of view, decrease friction and open the door to the possibility of harmony, or at least respectful disagreement.

Come Back Home!
Having cycled through the second and third perceptual positions - come back home. Come back to your first position self and your centre. It is from here that your communication is most engaging and compelling.

Case Study - Paul Marwaha
Paul Marwaha is an award-winning film and television cameraman. I was fortunate enough to work with him on several presentation courses. Paul's official role was to film the delegates as they gave their presentations. The trainers and delegates would then review the film for the purposes of feedback. In between presentations, we would do various warm-up and preparation exercises. When not filming, Paul would occasionally join in the exercises but more often than not he would sit quietly in the background taking in the general dynamic of what was happening in the room. Paul had been sitting in the background observing courses for a lot longer than I had been standing in the foreground running courses. He had seen a lot more trainers in action, with their different styles and approaches, than I ever had. What a fantastic resource! Any time I was feeling a little bit stuck and not quite sure what direction to head in, I would simply have a quick word with Paul. From his third position perspective he would accurately assess the atmosphere of the group and suggest a good exercise, the right words to say or simply recommend that great tradition — the tea break. Sometimes when my co-trainer was leading a group activity, I would just go and sit beside Paul and soak up the group dynamic from this third position vantage point. This became an anchor for me even when Paul was not around. Just sitting at the edge of the room, noticing the patterns, often gave me an idea of where to go next.
Keep on people-watching like Paul — it is a wonderful presenter's tool.

STATE YOUR GOALS IN POSITIVE TERMS

- Do you want to be able to speak with greater calmness and composure?
- Perhaps you would like to speak with more conviction and passion?
- Would you like to know how to construct a presentation more easily?
- Or maybe you are constantly involved in a process of continually developing your skills?

Whatever your goals, it is immensely helpful to state them in terms that are positive. It is easier to visualize what you want than what you do not want. Consequently, 'I want to be calmer and more composed' is preferable to 'I do not want to be frightened'. 'I want to be able to express my thoughts in a clear and systematic way' is preferable to 'I don't want my words come out in a jumble.'

Of course, it is also very important to formulate goals for your audience, e.g. 'I want the audience to be so stimulated by my presentation that they think about it all the way home.' This could lead to some more specific goals, e.g. 'I want the audience to be so stimulated by my presentation that they buy my product/service.'

Practical Exercise – State your goal

Sometimes people can find it very difficult to formulate a positive outcome, usually because they have been immersed in a limiting mind-set that has reduced their horizons. A simple tip for dealing with this is to describe your goal first in negative language — 'I don't want to be terrified while presenting' — then to describe it again in the exact opposite way — 'I want to be deliriously happy while presenting'. You can then start to fine tune: 'I want to be confident'; 'I want to be in tune with the audience'; 'I want to enjoy being in tune with my audience.' Keep adjusting until your stated goal makes you feel positive and relaxed.

- Chapter Four -

HOW COMMITTED ARE YOU?

'It is not enough to have knowledge; one must also apply it. It is not enough to have wishes; one must also accomplish.'
Johann Wolfgang Von Goethe

'Until one is committed there is hesitancy, the chance to draw back, always ineffectiveness. Whatever you can do, or believe you can, begin it. Boldness has genius, power and magic in it.'
W.N. Murray, The Scottish Himalayan Expedition, 1951

GO FOR IT!

Whatever your current level of skills, identify an opportunity for presenting that will require you to crank up your skills by a few notches. Not something that will make you panic but something that will stretch you a bit. Then put yourself on the spot. Set the date. Advertise the fact. Let it be known publicly.

There is nothing like potential embarrassment for mobilizing one's resources. Once you have set the date and advertised the fact, get your team to work on preparing you for the big event. Think of giving a presentation as a team sport, rather than a solo sport. You don't have a team? Behind every great woman or man, and their presentations, there are family, friends or colleagues.

Now practise the skills that will ensure that you do yourself justice. You have to do your training as part of the team.

Planning — Step One

a) Practise your centring regularly. There are more suggestions about how to approach this later in this chapter and in the following chapter.

b) Choose the subject for your presentation. You may already know what this is. For novel and fresh ways of presenting your subject, see Chapter 6.

c) Estimate how long it will take you to get ready to present this subject in public. How much time will you need for research, structuring, solo rehearsal, rehearsal with your team and finally public presentation? If you are the type of person who tends to be late for things, double your most optimistic estimate.

d) Open up your diary and find or create the necessary preparation and rehearsal time the subject for your presentation

Planning — Step Two

a) Do your research using all the means available to you

b) Start to structure and organize your material. Chapter 6 is full of suggestions about how to do this.

Planning — Step Three

Your message - the words of your presentation - is of paramount importance but the non-verbal component is also vital. To make sure that your words are seeds sown in fertile ground, you need to give sufficient time and attention to the non-verbal elements.

a) Allow sufficient time to plan the words and the non-verbal elements. Revise your original estimate of the time needed.
b) Centre and rehearse:
Call your muse on the move.
Do this in your 'in-between' moments, such as waiting in queues. Let your mind wander to your presentation.
Solo rehearse chunks of your presentation.
Practise three opening lines of your presentation. Practise three lines from the middle. And practise three closing lines. The emphasis here is on physical, spatial and vocal presence.
Do a solo run through of your whole presentation.
Rehearse the presentation with your team.
The team could be colleagues, family members or even dolls and teddy bears!
Do it for real!

Planning — Step Four
Get as much constructive feedback as possible before and after.

Expect to continue learning and improving, both consciously and deliberately, and unconsciously and spontaneously.
Most of us need to put in a bit of practice to get progressively nearer to that enviable state of connection between self, subject and audience.
Commitment is the vital link that will take you from that demotivating feeling of 'have to' present to the highly motivated place of 'wanting to' present.
So, what factors reduce motivation and commitment?

- Fear about presenting or some aspect of presenting
- The perceived size of the task
- Lack of self-belief
- 'Square peg in a round hole' syndrome — a poor fit between person and job.

To a greater or lesser degree, all of these commitment-reducing factors will influence and reinforce each other. The good news is that a change in any one of these areas will encourage change in all of the others.
The next few sections will show how to effect these changes.

Now be a bit more positive and consider what the commitment-increasing factors might be:

- Developing increased confidence about presenting or about aspects of presenting
- Cutting the task down into easy, bite-sized chunks
- Deliberately cultivating self-belief
- Developing a good fit between self and job.

KISS – Keep it Simple and Straightforward

'Everything should be made as simple as possible, but no simpler.'
Albert Einstein

Why is it that computer people have such a strong tendency to deluge their audience with information and, ultimately, send them to sleep?
I was discussing this question with a Vice President from an American company that has a strong international profile. The V.P. in question dealt with I.T. (Information Technology) people on a daily basis.
"A misplaced sense of generosity?" I suggested.
He replied, "They think that the more you give people the more they get. They haven't really become acquainted with the concept that.... less is more."
The great Napoleon Bonaparte was reputed to have rehearsed and simplified his speeches until the stupidest soldier in his army could understand exactly what he was saying.
I'm not actually suggesting that you reduce all your presentations to the lowest common denominator. A strategy I have frequently found useful is to rehearse to an audience that is intelligent but naive of the subject in question, i.e. colleagues, spouses, family, friends, etc. They will often ask you to clarify ideas and concepts that are blindingly obvious to you but impenetrable to others. This was an approach that Jack Welch, long time CEO of General Electric, espoused for himself and his senior management team.
This will help you to adopt and live the KISS principle - Keep it Simple & Straightforward. If you flag up beforehand that you will be having a question and answer session at the end, then you will be able to address more complex questions appropriately.
Be brave. Try it out. Watch the light bulbs switching on!

REDUCING FEAR & INCREASING CONFIDENCE

'It's a matter of ABC: When we encounter ADVERSITY, we react by thinking about it. Our thoughts rapidly congeal into BELIEFS. These beliefs may become so habitual we don't even realize we have them unless we stop to focus on them. And they don't just sit there idly; they have CONSEQUENCES. The beliefs are the direct cause of what we feel and what we do next. They can spell the difference between dejection and giving up, on the one hand, and well-being and constructive action on the other. The first step is to see the connection between adversity, belief, and consequence. The second step is to see how the ABCs operate every day in your own life.'

Sir Walter Scott

'Belief is a matter of customary muscle tension.'

F.M. Alexander

I love the above quote by Sir Walter Scott – it's so modern! Walter Scott really practised what he preached – he was a master at transforming his own personal adversity into abundant opportunity. As a little experiment, try putting the key words into Google and see what you come up with. You might find quite a few modern versions of 'ABC' out there but to my mind, none of them quite as succinct and pithy as Sir Walter Scott's.

The second quote is by F M Alexander, the originator, of the Alexander Technique. It was considered to be quite a provocative statement in the 1930s. Some people have suggested that he said it in order to shock. I, however, believe that he was perfectly serious about it — in Alexander's experience a rigidity of mind corresponded to a rigidity of body.

Try buying into the two quotes. Decide to treat them as if they were true. Believe that by changing your muscular reaction to adversity, or to the pressures of everyday work and life, you will also change, for the better, the consequences that arise from adversity.

How can you change your muscular reactions? How can you weaken the hold of a limiting belief? There are many possibilities.

Keep your head

In situations of real or imagined threat, a group of responses called the 'fight or flight' syndrome come into force. This syndrome acts by releasing hormones, including adrenaline, in the bloodstream. These hormones make the muscles more tense and speed up both breathing and heart rate. The muscles that connect shoulders, neck and head are often the first to contract in the fight/flight pattern, causing the head to be pulled back and down towards the body's centre of gravity. Blood flow is diverted from the surface and the core of the body to the muscles, with a consequent rise in blood pressure. In this situation a person's face will often drain of colour as the blood moves away from the skin surface.

Fortunately there are many ways of reducing and creatively channelling the energy of the fight/flight pattern to enhance your performance and communication skills. You will already be familiar with some of them from the previous chapter. We shall look at some additional, related strategies in this chapter. We shall also look at how these quick and effective personal resource boosters can massively enhance the use of your voice and body during presentations. If you are one of the lucky few that do not experience nerves, do try these techniques anyway - they are foundation techniques for using your voice and body to maximum effect.

Posture, Impact and Confidence

Your posture shapes your visual impact, modulates your voice and has a profound influence on how you think and feel.

How to 'wear your head' skilfully

People 'read' other people through eye contact and through scanning their facial expression. The relationship between head, neck and shoulders powerfully frames the facial expression – for better or worse. The easier and more expanded your head, neck and shoulder relationship is the more positive will be the impression you impart to others. It will also allow you to 'keep your head' and behave with greater calmness and assurance.

How to keep your head

The critical moment of starting to speak brings into play many inappropriate habits associated with the fight/flight reflex. The most common vocal habits are associated with audibly sucking or sniffing in

a breath before speaking. This sucking or sniffing action is associated with a tightening and narrowing of the airways.
This causes a dramatic increase in the contraction of muscle groups that have nothing directly to do breathing - the neck and throat muscles, shoulders, upper arms, upper chest and back - which leads to a visible displacement of head balance at the moment of breathing in.
A more general awareness of balancing the head easily and efficiently on top of your spine in the non-demanding moments of day-to-day life will help you to keep your head during the more pressurised times.
Because the head is so close to the voice box and the mouth, a better balance of your head and alignment of your spine will positively affect the way that you speak.

Practical Exercise - Breathing

Listen for any audible sucking or sniffing that you make while inhaling during normal speech. This habit will almost certainly be more exaggerated when you speak publicly.
Centre yourself and recite Sonnet 18 (Page 34) or another poem.
Allow your breath to return as smoothly, easily and quietly as possible between phrases. As an experiment try closing your lips between phrases – allowing the breath to return quietly and smoothly between phrases. Closing your lips between phrases is unrealistic for live presentation but extremely useful as an exercise.

The Weight of your Head

Consider that an average adult human head is about 10% of the total bodyweight – say 12 to 15 lbs. That's the equivalent of between two and three 5lb bags of potatoes balancing on top of your spine.

When I taught at the Arts Educational Drama School we had a lecture from a medical voice specialist. He told us that they were seeing an increasing number of patients with the combined symptoms of inflammation and hoarseness - symptoms more normally associated with heavy voice users such as teachers and actors. The difference was that these patients hardly spoke at all during their working day. Who were they? Computer operators with badly set up workstations. This was in the early 1990's.

Nowadays, we are all familiar with the sight of people peering into their laptop screen. The head, a tenth of the body weight, is pulling forward and downwards exerting pressure on the throat and compressing the ribcage.

It was clear that changing the workstation and the working posture was going to be an essential component of the voice therapy.

Rocking Stones

Rocking stones or Logan rocks are found throughout the world. Some of these large stones weigh more than 90 tonnes. They are so delicately balanced that the least touch causes them to gently rock. They are a fascinating natural phenomena.

Natural head balance is no less of a fascinating natural phenomenon.

Atlas Supports the Occiput

Your head balances on two tiny bony surfaces called the occipital condyles. Each condyle is roughly the size of your little fingernail and they are situated fairly centrally on the baseplate of your skull.

The top vertebra of your spine is called the Atlas, after the classical Greek God who was said to support the globe of the planet Earth. The globe of your skull, via the occipital condyles, balances delicately on the very pinnacle of the Atlas vertebra.

Delicate Levers

Because the skull is so beautifully balanced it doesn't require bulky muscle to either balance or to move. Your head is balanced and moved by groupings of slim muscles that work together to keep your head poised on top of your spine with a minimum of effort.

The Skull

Trace around the base of your skull until your fingers come to the soft, hollow-ish area just behind your jaw joint. Point your fingers, through your neck, towards each other. About 2.5 cm before your fingers would meet (if they could) is the approximate location of the atlanto-occipital joint, the place where the top of your spine joins the base of your skull.

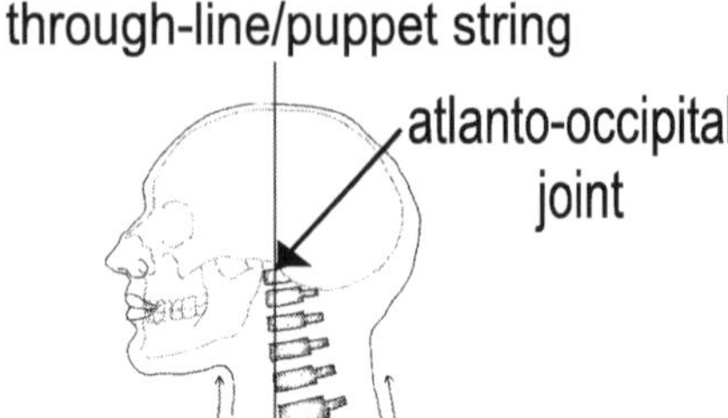

The Spine

The spine is longer and substantially thicker than most people realize. Its weight-bearing parts are located deep in the core of the torso. Understanding this fact significantly contributes to an enhanced sense of inner support. The lumbar section of the spine occupies at least a quarter of the depth of the body. The spine occupies at least a quarter of the depth of the ribcage and up to half the depth of the neck. By the time you add spinal muscles to the picture, the spine looks even more substantial, The spine is like a supremely well-jointed and muscular 'fifth limb', that stretches up from the tail-bone to support and balance the globe of the head within space.

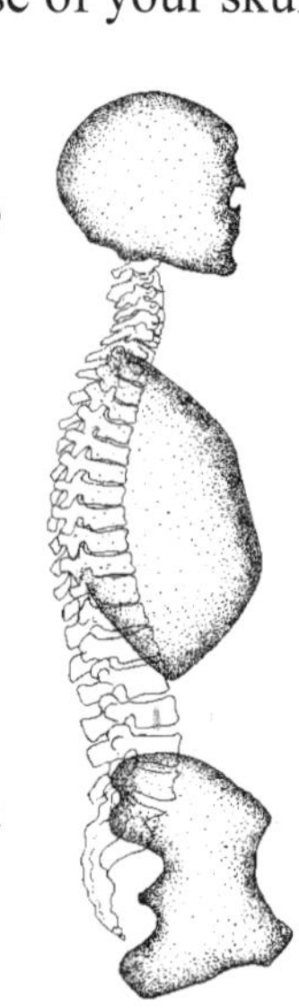

The 'Through Line'

American artist Todd Kline balances rocks on top of each other. His highest sculpture has been 17 rocks high. The resulting sculptures are often improbably asymmetrical. And yet they stay upright and balanced in winds of 15 miles an hour. Kline attributes this ability to create balance to perceiving the "Through Line" that runs straight through every object.

The top-heavy human body is also a masterpiece of the improbable art of balancing. With more than 200 bones and 600 muscles piled on top of a small foundation, we too manage to stay upright not only in high winds but also on very uneven and unstable surfaces.

To put this in a practical context, think of a puppet string attached to the top of your head that initiates the release of the neck muscles and the easy balancing of the head on top of a lengthening spine. If the puppet string is placed too far forward, your head tips back. Place the string too far back and the head tips forwards. If the puppet string is placed directly above the area where the spine joins the skull, the head will tend to come into an easy, level balance on top of the spine, which will encourage the spine to lengthen.

Practical Exercise - Your Puppet String/Through Line

With both hands, trace up from your atlanto-occipital area, directly past the ear-holes, until your fingers meet at the top of your head. Tap gently on this spot for a minute. Now bring your hands down to rest at your sides. You will probably still feel the sensation of the tapping for a few moments. This area, directly above the top of your spine, is where your imaginary puppet string attaches.

With the help of the imaginary puppet string, guide yourself into a state that is more balanced around your line of gravity (See Chapter 3 page 45). Do not make any muscular effort to change the way you are standing - let the puppet string do it for you.

It is useful to do this exercise with the help of a friend, or a mirror, as you might try at first to tilt your head forwards or to the side to meet your hand.

Keeping it Simple - Centre, centre, centre

Research from the University of Western Australia (Gucciardi and Dimmock) suggests that golfers who focus on holistic single word cues perform better under competition pressure than those who focus on the more complex instructions associated with a typical golf lesson. We can apply the same thinking to preparing for a presentation. Try saying the following phrases out loud:

I'm nicely centred
I'm beautifully grounded
My head is exquisitely poised on top of my spine
My shoulders are wide and open
My vision is wide and receptive.

Now condense the instructions:

I'm centred
I'm grounded
My head is poised
My shoulders and vision are wide.

Condense the instructions still further:

Centred
Grounded
Poised
Wide.

And still further:

Centre... centre... centre.

EMOTION, BREATHING AND YOUR VOICE

In the early 1940s, the surgeon William Faulkner carried out an experiment in which he measured his patients' physical responses to both stressful and pleasant thoughts. When his patients thought of something unpleasant, he noticed that the movement of their diaphragm became restricted, shallow and irregular. These breathing changes were accompanied by a corresponding tightening of the throat and negative changes in the characteristic of the patient's speaking voice. Conversely, when his patients thought of something pleasant, the movement of their diaphragm became expansive and regular and the levels of tension in the throat were reduced. All of this was accompanied by positive changes in the characteristics of their voices.

In the following exercise you can compare the effects that stressful and pleasant thoughts have on you and your voice. You will be recalling and reliving an example of each emotional state in turn. So please do make sure that the unpleasant one is quite mild. The pleasant one can be very pleasant indeed!

For more information and practical procedures about breathing, please see Chapter 13, 'A Word About Breathing'.

Exercise 1: Observing restriction

1. Think of a time when you felt mildly pressured and restricted. Remember this using your mind's eyes, ears and feelings — what you saw around you, what you heard and also what you felt. Stay fully in this state for a couple of minutes.
2. Now look around the room. Does it look any less bright or any less friendly than before? Do you feel taller or shorter? Do you feel wider or narrower? What size does your personal space seem to be (indicate this with your hands)?
3. Walk around the room. Is your walking lighter or heavier?
4. Vocalize an 'aahh' sound. How easy or difficult is it to vocalise?
5. Now introduce yourself to an imaginary audience:
   "Hello. My name is _________ and today I am going to speak to you about______."

Exercise 2: Observing and cultivating ease

1. Move and stretch to dissipate the effects of the last exercise.
2. Remember a time when you felt on top of the world. Recall and relive this experience — what you were seeing, hearing and feeling. Stay fully in this state for a couple of minutes and allow yourself to release your breath outwards for a little bit longer, slightly more slowly than you normally would. Can you allow your breath back in at an easy, unforced flowing pace? Let this top of the world feeling spread, little by little, across your whole body.
3. Look around the room again. Is it any brighter or friendlier now? Do you feel shorter or taller? Narrower or wider? How large is your personal space now?
4. Take a walk around the room. Is your walking heavier or lighter?
5. Vocalize an 'aahh' sound. Notice how your voice feels and sounds different from the first exercise.
6. Introduce yourself again to your imaginary audience.

You have just taken the first step in freeing your body and liberating your voice!
Ultimately it will become clear that your body, feelings and mind are part of one system. A change in any one of them - body, feelings or mind - will affect all the others.

THE SIZE OF THE PERCEIVED TASK

The larger a task is, the more it has to be broken down into easily attainable sub-tasks or chunks. Working on small chunks helps to bring the presenter/performer into the here-and-now and therefore more into their body, which is the foundation stone of the voice. Unlike daily life, where one activity slides into another, a presentation has a more clearly defined beginning, middle and end. This makes it easier to practise small, specific and manageable chunks at a time.

Your emotional state

When you have a presentation coming up, you may feel that you have simply got too much on your plate. This is usually linked to your personal state — physical, emotional and mental. When you are feeling low, the size of a task can expand dramatically in your mind and make you feel even more physically weighed down. On the other hand, when you feel awake and refreshed, tasks can seem a great deal smaller.

'At 40 I am beginning to learn the mechanism of my own brain. How to get the greatest amount of pleasure and work out of it. The secret is, I think, always so to contrive that work is pleasant.'

Virginia Woolf

Just how do you contrive that your work is always pleasant?

HASTEN SLOWLY AND PLEASANTLY.

Practical Exercise – Hasten slowly and pleasantly

1. Make a list of six things that you have to do.
2. Now make yourself very tense and imagine yourself doing the activities. How motivating is this? How committed do you feel? Tension often leads to fatigue and slump. Get yourself into a heavy, slumped state and imagine yourself doing the activities on your list.
3. Now take a minute or two to centre yourself and open up your sense of personal space. Think through item 1 on your list. Pause and refresh your centring for a few seconds. Now think through item 2. Pause and re-centre. Repeat until you reach the end of your list and centre yourself once again. You will be much more likely to see your iist of activities through to their conclusion when you approach them in this way.

Later in the chapter you will work on some bite-sized chunks of a whole presentation, i.e. the opening and closing remarks. You will practise them in a physically, spatially and vocally centred way. You will then identify some real-life situations in which to practise them so that they are available to you, ready and waiting, during more demanding presentations.

Chunking

Many aspects of centring help you to cut tasks down to size. Many of your centring exercises can be practised in the middle of boring day-to-day activities, such as waiting in a queue or at traffic lights. This will enable you to mentally rehearse chunks of your presentation. Not only will this cut down the frustration that is often felt at these moments, it will also positively affect your performance in the moments that follow.

A client of mine had been having some difficulty in establishing rapport with his customers. He found that he could improve his relationship with them by practising his new skills with the people who staffed his customers' reception desks:

"It was just a two or three minute walk from the station to my client's office. I walked slowly, remembering my centre, my width and my height. I was actually enjoying the hustle and bustle of central London all around me. I walked up to reception and waited while the receptionist finished a call. I smiled at her and told her my name and whom I had come to visit. Her face lit up and I was surprised when she said, "Oh, what a lovely clear voice you have! You've got no idea how many people mumble and rush when they come to reception!" I was slightly embarrassed, but mostly pleasantly surprised by this response. I wasn't even really thinking about my voice, but somehow the centring had worked its magic. The feeling continued in the lift and into my customer's office. The meeting with my customer was much more comfortable and constructive and I am glad to say it has continued that way. I've now turned this into part of my strategy. Reception can be an unrewarding job. If I make their day a little brighter the next time I arrive, I'll usually get a genuine smile and greeting from them. That warm reception sets me up for the business I am about to do."

Give some thought to the 'in-between' moments of your life - the places where, instead of becoming frustrated, you can practise your centring skills. Think also of low-risk places where you can practise making calm and composed entrances, followed by clear and centred introductions, greetings or opening lines. Do this regularly in low-risk settings and you will find it becomes increasingly available to you in more stretching situations.

SELF-BELIEF

In 1968, Rosenthal & Jacobson carried out an experiment designed to assess how the expectation of teachers would affect the performance of their pupils.

The children in the experimental group were a random mix of all levels - above average, average and below average - and were sorted into their respective primary grade levels. The children in the control group classes were sorted similarly for ability and age. The only difference was that the teachers of the experimental group classes were told to expect surprising gains in intellectual ability over the rest of the school year. At the end of the year, when they were all tested, the children in the experimental 'high expectation' group showed significantly greater intellectual gains than the children in the control group:

'Overall, the children from whom the teachers had been led to expect greater intellectual gain showed a significantly greater gain than did the children of the control group, thereby supporting the 'Pygmalion' hypothesis.' Rosenthal & Jacobson 1968

Although people often talk about the 'weight' of other people's expectations, they can also work in the opposite direction - the right kind of expectation can actually buoy the recipient up and help to set them on course. If you are fortunate you will have received this kind of support at some point in your life. There will be times, however, when you will have to do this for yourself. The next few pages will show you how.

Internal voices - talking your walk

A group is carrying out a simple exercise to be done in pairs.

One of the partners - the 'goal achiever' - chooses a simple task to carry out, such as walking across the room to pick up an object and then putting it down somewhere else. The other partner - the 'nag' - gives the moving partner the benefit of some critical instructions but in a nagging tone of voice, too fast for the person to assimilate. The instructions are couched entirely in negative language:

"Don't be off-centre! Don't be ungrounded! Don't tunnel your vision! Don't pull your head down! Don't shorten and narrow your back! Don't tighten your jaw, legs, arms! Don't hold your breath! Don't be slow!"

Imagine that you are either receiving or giving these instructions. How do they affect you physically, emotionally and mentally? You probably won't be surprised to hear that the goal achievers looked completely off-centre, ungrounded and stiff as they moved. Once they had completed their task they were tested for balance by the nag. Unsurprisingly they were quite unstable and wobbly. What is surprising is that when the goal achievers applied a balance test to the nags, the nags were also very wobbly and off-centre.

In the discussion afterwards, the achievers said that the instructions sounded and felt like this:

"OffcentreUngroundedTunnelyourvisionStiffenyourneckPullyourhead downHoldyourbreathBeslow!"

How did it make them feel?

"AAAAGH!" and ***"GGRRRRR!"***

And how motivated did it make them feel?

"FORGET IT!"

None of the nags took pleasure in their role. In fact, most of them said that they found the exercise had as negative an effect on themselves as it had on the goal achiever.

The nags were now transformed into 'coaches' and gave encouraging directions in a pleasant tone and with appropriate pacing:

"Take a moment to remember your centre ... Good... and as you remember your centre so you can also get more grounded... and allow your visual field to open and expand... And when you are good and ready you can walk across the room and move your object... Move at a pace that is comfortable to you... Your back is long and wide...head balancing easily on top of your spine... Excellent... Breathe smoothly and flowingly as you walk..."

On completing their task, they again tested each other for balance. This time they were quite stable, flexible and confident. Both coach and goal achiever were full of calm energy and ready for the next task on the agenda, whatever it may be.

What was the most significant part of the exercise? Apparently, the most valuable experience was that of being the coach. After all, if you could be nurturing, encouraging and motivating for someone else, why not be just as loving to yourself?

Practical Exercise – No nagging
The next time you have to give someone instructions, such as directions, try doing it with a warm, encouraging tone and with appropriate pacing. Keep your eyes and ears alive so that you can see and hear how they are responding. This will automatically affect the rate at which you speak and pause.

PERSON AND JOB — GETTING THE FIT RIGH

The general theme of this chapter has been about going from the feeling of 'having to present' to 'wanting to present'. This will be much easier if you are already doing a job that you want to do rather than feel you have to do. It is even more important to be able to get into a state where you want to present, despite being in a job that you are not entirely happy with. At the very least you can cultivate the 'want to' feeling in your presentation style, even if you are not entirely charmed with the presentation content. Use your presentations as an opportunity to prime yourself so that you are ready to take on your dream job when the occasion arises.

Case Study - Phyllis

Phyllis had spent many years working as a librarian for a particular employer. In the beginning it was the right job, in the right place, with the right people. Unfortunately, her conditions of employment deteriorated progressively over a number of years until it became the wrong job, in the wrong place, at the wrong time and full of very unhappy people. It had become so intolerable that Phyllis was strongly considering leaving the job without having alternative employment in place. Jobs for librarians were few and far between and, because she did not have a degree, Phyllis was not hopeful about her prospects at interview. This had the effect of diminishing her performance at the actual interview, so Phyllis decided to take a two-day presentation course.

When people work under the unhappy conditions described above, their self-esteem can often take a bit of a knock. During the first part of the course Phyllis was overly critical of her efforts during her presentations. She received firm encouragement from the trainer, who would brook no contradiction. Phyllis began to give herself the benefit of the doubt. She started enjoying herself more and her performance improved.

Shortly afterwards, Phyllis went for an interview at a high profile academic institution in Glasgow:

"I thought 'OK, Phyllis. This is your big chance so let's make the most of it. I'm determined that I am going to enjoy this interview. Centre yourself... Allow your spine to lengthen. Breathe out gently and

smoothly... I'm going to extend a very positive, calm feeling to the interviewers... In fact I'm going to interview them... I'm going to ask them some questions.' And I did feel calm. I did feel friendly. I did ask questions. And, even if I say so myself, I did a brilliant interview. I got the job and it's lovely. I found out later that I was the only librarian without a degree to get a job in this institution."

Not only did Phyllis get herself the ideal job but, once she had grasped the core principles for making presentations, she gathered increasing momentum and there was no stopping her.

- Chapter Five -

BETTER THAN WHAT?

'Attempt easy tasks as if they were difficult, and difficult tasks as if they were easy, in the one case that confidence may not fall asleep, in the other that it may not be Dismayed.'
Baltasar Gracian

'… remember that nervousness doesn't show one tenth as much as you feel. If you are slightly scared, you won't appear to be scared at all. And if you're very scared, you'll appear slightly scared. And if you're absolutely bloody terrified, you will only seem slightly bothered.'
David Nixon

USING YOUR SKILLS

We all know people who are great speakers over a cup of coffee or on the phone, at home or informally in the office - fluent, earnest, fresh-thinking, witty and passionate. Yet put that person in front of an audience, and their verbal facility disappears.

This, in its own way, is an automatic response. Although the adrenaline-fuelled reaction is remarkably similar from person to person, the circumstances that stimulate it vary tremendously. For some people it is not the size of the audience but their status that is important. Presenting to a peer group will terrify some, while presenting to those with greater authority or influence scares others. Size is a significant factor for many but there is not much agreement on what constitutes a large audience - ten, twenty, two hundred? For others, small audiences trigger fear. Some people feel more comfortable presenting than they do with ordinary social interaction.

A little word about adrenaline

People can forget or draw a blank mid-presentation on information they know perfectly well. Momentarily they stop knowing what they know. They may curse themselves afterwards for forgetting something that seems entirely obvious.

Why? Adrenaline is designed to keep you safe by making you act quickly. It dampens down thinking because in many cases thinking is too slow.

By remaining centred you will also be calm enough to retrieve all the necessary material from your memory banks. But it can get even better than that. With practice it is possible to get a delicious blend of adrenaline on the one hand with calmness on the other. In this state you can start to know things that you didn't know you knew... It's called creativity. It's also called thinking on your feet.

We are all intensely individual and deeply unique but we are all wrought from the same basic ingredients - body, voice, language and awareness of other people. Even quite minor adjustments to the proportions of these ingredients can lead to huge changes in the way that we feel, express ourselves and engage with others, without compromising our individuality.

How can you create a response to presentation nerves that will allow you to have the same quality of rapport with an audience as you have during your best moments such as informal conversation?

In this chapter, you will work on the non-verbal, physical, spatial and vocal elements of rapport-building, including:

- Using your eyes and ears to observe the body language and voice of other individuals
- Adjusting your body language and voice to gain rapport with other individuals
- Transferring individual rapport skills into audience contexts
- Eye contact
- Noticing potential friends and allies in the audience
- Taking ownership of your space
- Adjusting your personal space according to the size and type of your audience
- Strengthening your competence and confidence with challenging people and situations
- Using feedback effectively.

Confidence or Assurance?

The legendary David Thomas, founder of cult American band Pere Ubu, is scathing about an aspect of my professional life – confidence coaching. Why? Well, he knows that many musicians, actors and public speakers give the most superlative performances despite experiencing high levels of ‘nerves’.

He speaks with authority having released 40 albums over the past 40 years and doing musical tours of Europe and America on a yearly basis.

“It doesn't matter what you feel,” he argues, “as long as you ‘behave’ with assurance on stage then the audience will believe in you.” He states that this in turn will bring forth your best possible performance. This is an interesting point of view. I don't agree with it wholeheartedly but I respect it. Behave with assurance on stage and you give the audience confidence in you. They relax because they sense you are in control. This, in turn, reinforces your assured behaviour and amplifies feelings of self-confidence. Which begs the question - who does the confidence belong to? You? The audience? Both?

Feeling a little bit calmer and more centred in the first place will help you to behave with that desirable level of assurance right from the outset. Confidence and assured behaviour become mutually reinforcing - a virtuous circle.

HUMAN MIRRORS

Rapport can be developed physically by mirroring a person's body language - arms, legs, posture, shoulders and face. It can be developed vocally by reflecting the pitch, rhythm, volume and tempo of someone's voice. Physical and vocal mirroring can help put the person you are speaking to at ease. It also develops your sensory acuity - you will see and hear the other person much more accurately and clearly, if you work on these rapport skills with a trusted partner, you can then transfer them into group-based presentations of any size.

Practical Exercise - Mirroring

Work with a trusted partner for this exercise.

1. Copy precisely the posture, hand and arm gestures, foot and leg positions, head, neck and shoulder carriage, and facial expressions of your partner as they speak.
2. Now copy your partner's gestures in a more subtle manner. For example, large arm movements could be mirrored with much smaller but similar hand movements. This minimalist mirroring allows you to remain centred and aligned with yourself and yet build a bridge to your partner at the same time.
3. Do the opposite of your partner - for example, when he or she leans left, you should lean right.

Mirroring in daily life

Mirroring is a natural process. It is one reason why family members or close friends tend to stand, walk and talk in similar ways.

A note of caution does have to be sounded here, however. We all know individuals who drain our energy or jangle our nerves despite being the loveliest of people. Because they are approachable and nice, it is easy to get hooked into their prevailing destructive emotional state, which can drag you in a negative direction.

This also works the other way with positive people with high levels of energy. We hook into and get drawn up towards their higher energy level and emotional state and walk away from them feeling refreshed and happier. This is the kind of strategy you need to adopt for presenting to groups - hook your audience verbally and non-verbally and start to gently open up the appropriate energy and mood for the occasion.

Vocal mirroring

Remember some of the vocal characteristics from Chapter 2 (page 29):

- Volume
- Pace and rhythm
- Articulation
- Pitch and variation
- Resonance
- Silence and pause.

Think of the origin of each of these types of voice: do they seem to come from the throat, the chest or the head? How would you need to hold your body to make that sound yourself?

Once you have begun to develop an ear for the variations in the ways that other people speak, you will find it easier to mirror different vocal styles.

EYE CONTACT

As with many other aspects of presenting, there are no hard and fast rules concerning eye contact. There was a time, not so long ago, when popular advice to presenters or interviewees was 'Make sure you give good eye contact'. All too often this could turn into an uncomfortable battle of wills with the first person to break eye contact feeling like the loser.

It is quite normal to make and break eye contact. If you watch any conversation between two people who are reasonably comfortable with one another you will see this happen in its own, almost dance-like, rhythm. Most people find it disconcerting if eye contact is not held for long enough or is held for too long. The state of mind of the person giving or receiving the eye contact also influences the comfort factor positively or negatively.

As a general rule, the more centred you are, the more pleasant or acceptable your quality of eye contact will be. The guidelines for new instructors of the martial art Aikido, state that a teacher should have 'soft and friendly eyes'. This advice holds good for most presentation circumstances, as it tends to increase your authority rather than diminish it. If your eye contact is hard, yours listeners are likely to become less receptive. If your eye contact is soft yet direct, your listeners will soften and your information will be absorbed more readily by their brains and memory.

Imagine that there is a triangle on the face of the person you are looking at or speaking to. The base of the triangle spreads from the bridge of the nose to the edges of the eyebrows. The sides sweep down both sides of the face, past the corners of the mouth, to meet at the point of the chin.

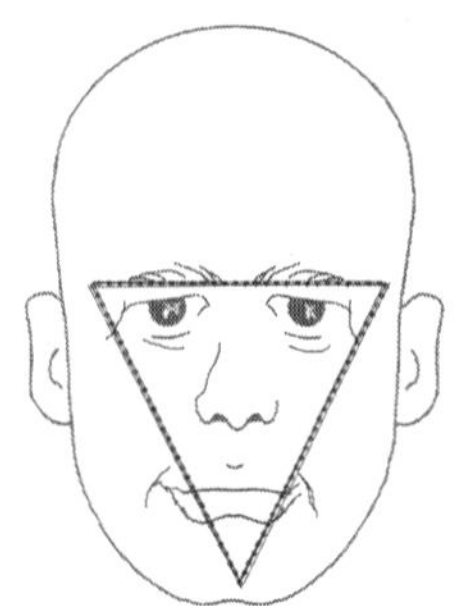

If you look anywhere within this triangle, the recipient will still feel as if you are looking into their eyes.

How long should eye contact last?

You should maintain eye contact for about the length of a spoken phrase, then move on to someone else, again for the length of a phrase. This will be felt by your audience to be a natural and personal length

of time, especially if it is coupled with a centred, calm speaking pace. Try practising this strategy while reciting Sonnet 18 (Page 32).
A good strategy when giving a presentation is to find a person on your left, on your right and in the middle of your audience to talk to. Deliver one phrase to the eye triangle of the person on your left, one to the right and one to the person in the middle. Keep going like this, gradually make contact with more people until you get a good sense of your audience as a whole.

Eye contact starts at the feet

Presenters often give an unequal spread of eye contact because their feet, when standing, are not placed symmetrically towards the audience. If your feet are parallel to one another or the toes of each foot are slightly turned away from each other, it is possible for the whole body, and therefore your eye contact, to turn equally from one side of the audience to another.

Symmetrical feet help to open your sightlines

If, however, one foot is turned in the same direction as the other, the whole body and sweep of the eyes will turn in the direction of the most outwardly turned foot.

Asymmetrical feet restrict sightlines

Sight lines

It is good practice to check your sight lines in your presentation venue before your audience arrives. Make sure that, wherever you may be sitting or standing to deliver your presentation, you can take in the whole audience using your peripheral vision. This should require no or minimal head turning. Stand or sit in the most central position possible in relationship to where the audience will be sitting. If you find that it is not possible to take in the whole of the audience area, move backwards until you can. If possible, move the seating to achieve the same effect. This will give you a sense of taking control of your surroundings and will make you look more at home.

ENERGY APPROPRIATE TO THE VENUE

Diligently using the methods in this book may well lead you to having a larger-than-life presence. Be careful! A larger-than-life presence may work in a 1000-seater theatre. The same presence in a small office or venue may blast people out of their seats and completely turn them off. Adjust your presence to suit the audience and venue.

GET TO KNOW YOUR AUDIENCE

When you are presenting, try to strike up a rapport with your audience before the session begins, for example over morning coffee. Apart from the usual conversation, this is an opportunity to gather useful information from participants or, where appropriate, to give them an outline of your presentation.

Your friends and allies in the audience

It is worth remembering that the vast majority of any audience are on your side. They have come to be enriched, informed or entertained in one way or another. This fact was consciously used in nineteenth-century theatre and opera productions. The head of a theatre company would hire a group of distinguished looking individuals - known as the claque - and ‘plant’ them throughout the audience. During the performance, they would make appropriate noises of approval and would launch into generous and lusty applause, sparking the rest of the audience into an equally enthusiastic response.

In any audience, there is already a claque waiting for you. The simple fact is that many people are natural smilers and nodders. These people are the members of your naturally occurring claque — all you have to do is notice and acknowledge them.

The identification of your claque can be carried out before you give your presentation. If your presentations are carried out in hotels for example, you can sit in the lobby and watch the people who are going to attend. When you begin to present, notice (using your peripheral vision) the natural smilers and nodders in your audience. Mark out three smilers and nodders — one to your left, one to your right and one in the centre. Address your first remarks to these three people.

With practice this will become second nature. You will be able to walk in, mark out your claque, acknowledge them with an almost invisible nod or smile and launch smoothly and easily into your presentation.

Case Study – James Lawley

James Lawley, psychotherapist, management trainer and founding member of the Central London NLP Practice.

"I have used the idea of a claque in the audience on many occasions. I now make it a point to make contact with people as they arrive, preferably by talking personally to them or, if this is not possible, by welcoming them all. At the very least, I try to make eye contact and smile. When I am being introduced before a presentation, I will seek out the people in the audience from whom I received the greatest response and attempt to acknowledge them with a smile or a nod. This helps me to create rapport and gives me a sense of connectedness with those individuals. I have found that if I consider these people to be 'light sources', radiating warmth to the people sitting immediately around them, my sense of connection expands during the presentation to include the whole audience."

FEEDBACK - ELECTRONIC AND PERSONAL

Reviewing your presentations frequently, even in small chunks, will help you pick up on those areas that are going well and those that need some work. You will become aware of those areas that you have omitted to cover. You might like to keep a note of these things in a notebook or audio recording. Lay yourself open to inspiration.
The use of video cameras to record and review performance is a feature of many presentation skills courses. Cameras can be absolutely brutal in highlighting the areas where you need to do some more work but they also frequently highlight those areas in which you are unconsciously exceeding your own expectations.
Nowadays we are spoilt for choice with so many devices offering video feedback - camcorders, mobile phones, iPads etc. Valuable as video feedback is, it can be fiddly and impractical for day-to-day use, e.g. if you don't have someone to film you you'll need a tripod to mount the device. You will also need to work out the sight-line borders of the camera and limit your movements accordingly.
While at home, or while out and about, a hand-held digital or tape recorder is a fine, inexpensive and portable alternative. If you prefer something of a very high digital quality, a mini-disc recorder is an excellent investment. The beauty of these voice recorders is that you can choose to either move around or stand still as you present.

But I hate the sound of my voice when it's recorded!

Just about everyone absolutely detests the sound of their recorded voice. Why does the voice that sounds so resonant inside your head sound so awful when it's played back? Accept and like yourself and your voice. Listen to some well-known TV and radio presenters. Do they all speak in a groomed, eloquent way? The medium is saturated with quirks, idiosyncrasies and speech impediments of every kind.

- Chapter Six -

STRATEGIES AND TECHNIQUES

'The room was hushed,
The speaker mute,
He'd left his speech
In his other suit.'
Kenneth McFarland, Eloquence in Public Speaking

'Stand up, speak out and don't bump into the furniture.'
Noel Coward

GENERATING YOUR CONTENT

Research over the past thirty years, shows that the two sides of our brain function in different but complementary ways. The left cerebral hemisphere specialises in tasks of a more linear/verbal nature - arithmetic, grammar, logic, etc. In contrast, the right cerebral hemisphere specialises in more artistic or pattern based tasks - rhythm, texture, colour, pattern, shape, etc. It is now widely acknowledged that we need the functions of both these hemispheres, working in harmony, to carry out even the simplest activities.

For example, think of how you recognize an acquaintance. Recognising their face is done by the pictorial right brain, remembering their name is a function of the verbal left brain. So what relevance does this have for writing a presentation?

Right brain: The Creative Generator

For the purposes of constructing a presentation, think of the right cerebral hemisphere as the creative generator of the material that you wish to present, like a team of investigative and creative journalists. The left hemisphere is the editor/organiser who gives coherent shape to the apparent chaos of the day's breaking news. To the outside observer, the flow of journalists in and out of the building, or the flow of their phone calls, faxes and emails, may look chaotic and disordered. Without further sorting of the articles, there is not a coherent newspaper. The flow of activity radiates out to the world and the gathered information floods back into the centre.

The biggest obstacle that many people face when writing a presentation is in trying to get it all down on paper in the correct logical sequence - beginning, middle and end - before the creative generator has been to work, i.e. before they have formulated all their raw ideas. Premature logical ordering of the material can create ‘log jams’ on the paper as you suddenly remember important points that you have left out. Frustration, the waste-paper bin and a desire to give it all up start overflowing!

It is much easier to first let the right brain get to work on the task of generating material and then let the left brain structure it into a logical and understandable sequence. Write down all your ideas in a way that suits you, then start to structure them.

Left brain: the Editor/Organiser

Having generated some ideas, you can now begin to order them into a linear and understandable sequence. Number each idea in order of priority. Now break down each idea into a key word or phrase. Use these as a prompt for your presentation.

Key words

Key words act like easily identifiable landmarks guiding you - the presenter - to your ultimate destination. These landmarks can liberate you from needing a verbatim text of your presentation. Presenters who use a series of key words end up with a better comprehension and memory of their material than those who slavishly stick to reading their material, word by word, from a text or script.

The speaker who simply reads out their presentation has to have their face and eyes pointing into the text most of the time, which reduces their visual impact and audibility.

Evocative key words, on the other hand, directly push the presenter's memory buttons, allowing the speaker to keep their eyes and face pointing in the direction of the audience. This enhances their visual impact, makes their voice more audible and leads to a much more compelling presentation.

Greater visual contact also allows a presenter to make a moment-by-moment assessment of how the audience is responding to the presentation and to adjust his or her behaviour accordingly.

Mind Maps

Mind Maps (organically organised keywords) were popularised by Tony Buzan, the learning methods pioneer. Tony Buzan was a regular visitor at the School of Alexander Studies when I was training to become a teacher of the Alexander Technique. We, the students, were extremely fortunate to receive tuition from Tony Buzan and his assistants. Constructing Mind Maps to prepare presentations, and books, has become an abiding approach.

Here is a Mind Map I used in the preparation of this book:

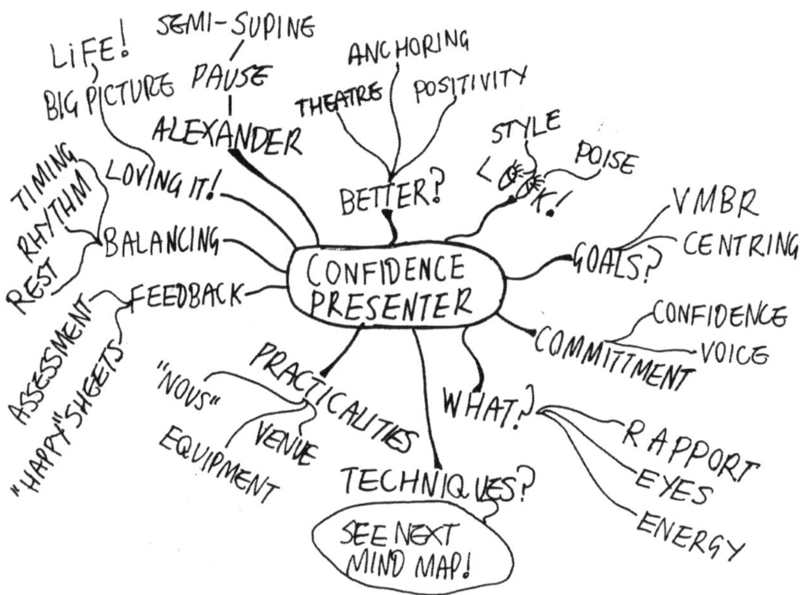

The 'branch lines' nearest to the centre represent the chapters. The chapters progress clockwise from 'Better?' at 12 o'clock to 'Techniques?' at 6 o'clock, 'Feedback' at 9 o'clock, etc.
The lines extending from these branches represent a selection of the individual chapter content. I usually enhance the immediacy of the Mind Map with coloured pens, doodles and pictures.

Index cards

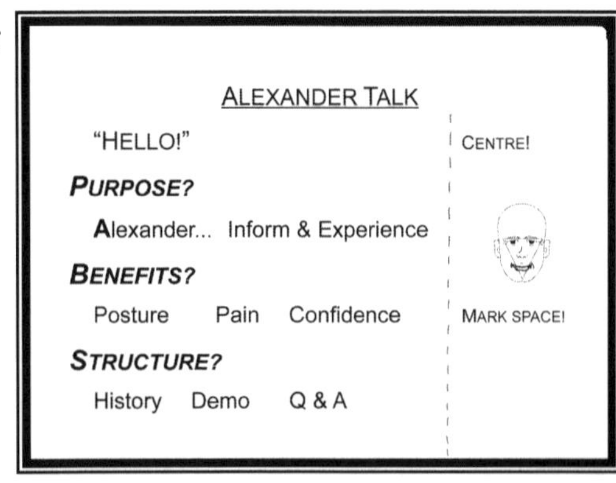

A useful way of arranging your material is to write each key word down in large capital letters on an index card. You can place any additional instructions, e.g. 'pause and centre' or a smiley face reminding you to smile at the audience, on the side of the card.

Index cards are much less intrusive than the standard sheet of paper. They do not rattle loudly in your hand and show the audience how nervous you truly are! They can be held unobtrusively at your side as you speak. They are also small enough to be kept in your pocket until required.

If left to their own devices however, index cards have a nasty habit of rearranging themselves into a totally incomprehensible order, especially if you drop them mid-presentation! For this reason it is a good idea to use a paper punch and treasury tags. Make a hole with the paper punch at the top left-hand corner of your index cards and thread the treasury tag through the holes. This will keep your precious notes in order through even the most demanding presentations.

Practical Exercise – Key Words

Break your presentation into key words and deliver it to an imaginary audience.

WILL ANYONE REMEMBER YOU?

To ensure the best possible audience recall of your subject, avoid delivering 'A Presentation'. Instead try delivering lots of little presentations, interspersed with related audience activities and breaks. If you want your audience to remember what you have actually said, you will need to say it in a way that suits the natural peaks and troughs of the average person's attention span.

Typically, people will recall more material from the beginning and end of a presentation and less from the middle. The longer a presentation is without significant changes of style, the less you can expect your audience to remember.

Changes of style, audience involvement and breaks create more opportunities for greater total recall of your message.

STRUCTURING A PRESENTATION

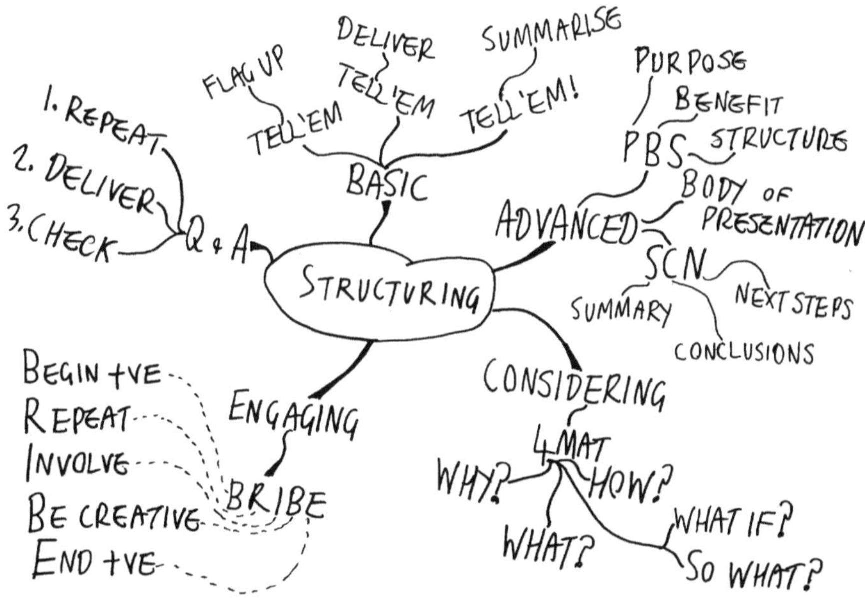

A Texan revivalist preacher was asked for the secret of his great success. After thinking deeply for a few moments, he gave the following reply:

> *"First I tell them what I am going to say.*
> *Then I say it.*
> *And then I tell them what I have just said."*

This is excellent advice that can be profitably used by any presenter. It has stood the test of time and is deservedly popular:

1. Tell the audience what you are going to say

Give them an outline of the content of your presentation. Make it simple - no more than three or four points. For example:
"Good evening ladies and gentlemen (or other appropriate greeting). Tonight I am going to speak to you about F.M. Alexander and the history of his discoveries. I will then give a demonstration Alexander

Technique lesson to a member of the audience. I will conclude my presentation by answering any questions that you may have."

2. Then say it

Deliver the content of your presentation, including demonstrations, questions and answers.

3. Tell them what you have just said

Conclude your presentation by summarising your three or four key points. Thank your audience for their attendance. This will bring your presentation to a clean end and avoid that uncomfortable feeling of uncertainty that often accompanies poorly concluded presentations.

4. Next steps

Encourage your audience to follow up your presentation by offering them some next steps:

"That concludes my presentation for this evening. Thank you for your attendance. For those of you who wish to find out more, there are leaflets on the table by the door... you may contact me at my office... I will remain in the room for another ten minutes. Please feel free to approach me."

Introductions: purpose, benefit and structure

A good system for introducing presentations is **PBS: Purpose, Benefit and Structure.** Here is an example from a talk that I recently gave on the Alexander Technique.

Purpose "Good evening ladies and gentlemen. My name is Alan Mars and tonight I have come to talk to you about the Alexander Technique."

Benefits "As well as helping with bad backs, stiff necks and so on, the Alexander Technique is very useful for helping actors to control stage stress and to harness the 'buzz' factor during performance."

Structure "First of all I will give you a short biography of F.M. Alexander and how he made his discoveries. Then I will do a few short demonstration lessons with members of the audience. And finally, I will answer any questions that you may have."

The PBS structure above has been set out in a fairly mechanical way for ease of instruction. For the actual delivery, it can be a lot more fluid and conversational in feel.

The End: Summary, Conclusions and Next Steps
A good way to round off a presentation is through SCN:
Summary, Conclusions and Next Steps.

Summary "So we've had the history of F.M. Alexander; we've done a hands on demonstration with some members of the audience and finally we had some very interesting questions."

Conclusions "We've heard how the technique helped Alexander with his breathing problems on stage and we've seen how the technique improved the way our volunteers used their voice in a Shakespeare text. Please do keep practising the exercises —you'll get more acting jobs if you do."

Next steps "For those of you who want to ask questions privately or who would like details of future training courses, I will be in the room for another 15 minutes. Please feel free to approach me. My cards are on the table at the back."

Both of the structuring formats above are extremely clear and easy to follow. They may seem somewhat rigid but, as with any technique, easy practice makes for an easier, and more natural sounding, delivery.

Case Study – Cheryl Winter
Cheryl Winter is a freelance Team Facilitator who was formerly a FCIPD Abbey National training consultant. In the following section she explains the 4Mat system which she has devised for structuring presentations.

A Structure for Presentations - The 4MAT System

Why do I use it?

The 4Mat system captures the flow of my presentation with 4 simple questions – no mnemonics or catchy buzz words – just some plain long established questions that we often want the answer to, and indeed we often ask!

For me, the discovery of this model came during a wonderful project with Boots back in 2001. The HR team wanted me to train new managers in team facilitation. The model worked with such simplicity and grace that as my project continued, I soon discovered the joy of working with something so straightforward, yet effective.

What is it?

The model is 4 questions:

- Why?
- What?
- How?
- What if? /So What?

The model itself was developed by Bernice McCarthy and based on research of school children in the 1970's. McCarthy noticed that some children wanted reasons. They habitually asked the question "why?" Others wanted facts – "what?" questions, "where do they come from?", "what is it called?", etc.

Some were very pragmatic and wanted to know "how does it work?", "what does this do?"

The rest wanted to explore the future consequences- "what would happen if I…?"

From research we know that we maintain our preferred style of learning into adulthood; one style is more comfortable than the others in our way of working:

- Why? – Discussions
- What? – Teaching
- How? – Coaching
- What if/So what? – Self discovery

How do I apply the 4MAT model to presentations?

I start off by answering all four questions myself:

1. **Why do they need to know this material? What's in it for them? Why should they listen?** To achieve this I will often include a summary of what the presentation will include. I consider my audience and their background, and link my presentation material into their environment. I may use a theme from the news to demonstrate why my subject is appropriate right now.
2. **What does this 'thing' actually do? Where does it come from? Who is the author or owner?** I may give some history, yet I tend to keep this session brief, I see this more for the 'theorists' in my audience, yet nevertheless it is an important section
3. **How the presentation session will run? How can it work for them?** For example, will the audience be involved and discuss points arising from the presentation? **How can they use this back in their work place?** Will it be a telling session or an experiential session (this depends on the time I have for my presentation)? **How can the subject work for the audience? How does the model work?** In this section I may include a demonstration with a member of the audience.
4. **What if / So what?** I help my audience to cast their gaze into the future. To ponder on how the particular subject can be applied in different contexts and the consequences, its flexibility and diversity of application. This can become quite creative. How can the audience find out even more, hand outs, further reading, workshops I may run in the future? I like to leave them wanting more so they will come and ask at the end "how does this work?" or "could I use this with other clients/children/ teachers?".

Further advantages of the 4MAT style

How else do I use the 4Mat style? I use this model to introduce my training courses, or at the start of each individual session within a training course. It has the dual effect of painting the big picture for the audience and also gives sufficient clarity for the 'details' people too. The model is given high profile throughout the Practitioner and Master Practitioner Modules of Training Attention Ltd, where I am an Associate Partner. My marketing flyers are also set out in this way to capture the attention of my prospective clients. I use it with clients in my individual coaching practice to help those who wish to improve their presentation skills!

My daughter uses it in her homework when designing posters for subjects such as History or Art. She uses it in literacy classes to create debating letters. She uses it in conjunction with Mind Maps to kick start the research process.

The process itself links to other learning style theories:

4MAT	**Kolb**	**Honey and Mumford**	**Jung (Myers Briggs**
Why?	Abstract	Reflector	Introvert
What?	Concrete experience	Activist	Extrovert
How?	Active experimentation	Pragmatist	Feeler
What if?	Reflective observation	Theorist	Thinker

Bribery - without the corruption

This format draws heavily on the research of Tony Buzan and Michael Gelb. Presenting in this format will radically increase your audience's recall of the material you are delivering. Audience recall tends to be highest for the material delivered at the beginning and ending of a presentation. Make the most of this by delivering powerfully and memorably.

Audience recall is at its lowest in the middle of a presentation. Break your presentation into smaller sections. Recall is enhanced by involvement. Get them moving, interacting with each other, questioning, etc., and the recall will soar.

In other words, leave nothing to chance. Don't live in doubt about the outcome of your presentations. BRIBE your audience.

B **Begin Positively and Powerfully**
Make full use of posture, voice and personal space.
Give an overview of your presentation.

R **Repeat Your Main Points**
In varying ways, repeat them at least three times.

I **Involve Your Audience**
Use current events, questions and multi-sensory language.

B **Be Creative**
Use stories, comparisons and alliteration.

E **End Positively and Powerfully**
Make full use of posture, voice and personal space.
Make a short summary of your presentation.
Conclude clearly and powerfully.

Practical Exercise – BRIBE

B Begin Positively and Powerfully

Use posture, centring and your voice.
Give an overview of your presentation.
Remember that audience recall is at its peak at the beginning and end of a presentation, so make it count.

R Repeat Your Main Points

'We ought to do more of that... We ought to do more of that... We ought to... We ought to... We should do more of that... I urge you to think about that. . Think about this as you go home tonight...So that's what I want you to think about.'

The above quotes are from Bill Clinton's keynote speech 'The Struggle for the Soul of the Twenty-first Century'. In this speech, Clinton took a long hard look at the positive and negative aspects of where the major Western powers had come from, where they were now and the possible futures. The speech looked at the hard realities that we all will have to face. It also celebrated real, life-enhancing progress in business, health, education and human rights. And he asked everyone to consider the significant difficulties and opportunities that almost certainly lay ahead for ourselves and for future generations. Each time he repeated or varied one of the above phrases, he drove his message home. The speech was global and covered past, present and future but much of the time came down to simple, common sense recommendations.

I Involve your audience

Use audience involvement and activities where you break into groups or pairs.
KISS - Keep it short and sweet! Audience involvement works best when the audience is awake. Reading your presentation aloud from a script will take about twice as long as reading it silently. Presenting it to an audience will take about twice as long again. Time it in advance with a friend or colleague!

Whenever possible or appropriate, use inclusive language - ‘we’, ‘us’ and ‘our’.
Use questions - rhetorical and Q&A sessions.
Use multi-sensory language. People think differently: some are predominantly visual thinkers while others are more auditory or feeling.
Use references to current events where appropriate.

B Be Creative

Use illustrative stories and anecdotes with different times, places, characters, events and objects.
Use comparisons - a good way to present statistical information.
Introduce alliteration - ‘Short, sharp shock’, ‘Right customer, right product, right time.’

E End Positively and Powerfully

Use your posture, voice and personal space.
Make a short summary of your presentation and outline next steps.
Conclude clearly and powerfully.

QUESTION AND ANSWER STRATEGY

Question and answer time for many presenters is the most relaxing and stimulating part of the presentation - perhaps because the interaction is more like the dynamics of a normal conversation. Here are some tips to ensure that it goes well:

Repeat out loud or paraphrase the question that you've just been asked. And then check with the questioner that you have understood the question correctly. Why? Repeating the question achieves several objectives:

1. It gives you a short but extremely valuable amount of thinking space to clarify your answer.
2. Questioners do not always phrase their questions in a clear and audible voice. By repeating the question you are ensuring that the whole audience hears – especially those at the back of the room.
3. Presenters do not always understand the question correctly. If you've understood the question correctly the questioner will nod, smile or indicate verbally or non-verbally that you've understood.

This will save you the embarrassment of answering a question that hasn't actually been asked!

Once you have got the non-verbal go-ahead reply to the audience as a whole. It's good if you can do this systematically by starting with someone at the other end of the room. Work your way back, person-by-person and phrase-by-phrase, so that you finish your answer with the original questioner. This is important because:

1. If you only address your reply to original questioner they become centre-stage and may feel self-conscious and will be unlikely to absorb your reply.
2. The rest of the audience may feel somewhat ignored and become disengaged from what you're saying.
3. You increase your general stage presence by demonstrating your ability to engage the whole audience.

Check verbally and non-verbally with the questioner that the answer has been understood. Assuming it has, you can then move on to address further questions. If the answer hasn't fully satisfied, you may wish to clarify and then repeat the above procedure.

STYLE

Many presenters, teachers and lecturers have a habit of communicating their material in an overly verbal and linear way. This attempt to convey maximum information is done with the best of intentions but the presenter on this path may, sadly, send 75 per cent of their audience to sleep, as even the most linear and logical person thinks in a rich and colourful way:

1. In pictures - large and small . . . still pictures . . . moving pictures in black and white. . . in colour. . . in a variety of shades. Many people have a personal vision. Certain groups share a vision.

2. In words and sentences — in different tones of voice... *fast* & s l o w... **LOUDLY!!!** and *quietly* in just the same way as they speak in different tones, speeds and volumes.

3. With feelings and emotions - gut feeling... feelings of commitment... heartfelt feelings.

4. With sensations, movements and qualities - smooth... rough... silky... light... **heavy**...

To a greater or lesser degree, most people use a combination of visual, auditory, tactile and feeling/emotional thinking. An audience respond to your words, voice and actions with their own unique combination of multi-sensory thought associations.

An overly linear presentation may plunge your audience into boredom. They will try to escape from this physically unpleasant state through mind wandering, while the more conscientious members of your audience will try to 'concentrate' on what you are saying.

The job of a presenter is to magically evoke pictures, sounds and feelings in full, three-dimensional colour within the brains of the audience. The more pictures, colour, tone, texture and feeling quality in your presentation, the greater your audience's engagement and recall will be, and the more they will be inspired, moved or motivated. The next few exercises will increase the sensory richness conveyed by your speech and gestures.

Air Sculptures

Most people spontaneously paint or sculpt pictures in the air with their hands and arms during the course of an absorbing conversation. For some people, the unfamiliarity or tension of a formal presentation can interfere with this natural ability. Other people continue sculpting the air but fail to amplify their gestures enough to take account of the needs of a larger group.

Case Study - Dave

Dave is a representative of a firm that specializes in alternative holidays. He started a presentation by describing a beautiful holiday island:

"The sea is blue and usually very still. The beaches are beautiful and very clean. In the late afternoons there are classes in yoga."

This had very little impact on the group as they felt that he had just read a beautiful but uncompelling list. As he continued, he began to use gesture more expansively:

"Imagine a perfectly still mirror-like blue sea (Dave made a smooth, round, horizontal gesture indicating the still mirror-like quality) spread out in front of you (Dave spread arms out wide and gazes to the sea's horizon). You lie down and relax on the golden sands (made a reclining gesture with his hands and changed to present tense). Later on you do some nice relaxing yoga (Dave did a combined yoga stretch and yawn)."

This time Dave's voice took on a much more relaxing and hypnotic quality. Everyone agreed that his presentation was more compelling and relaxing.

Perhaps one of the most interesting points that the above examples draw out is the connection between voice and movement. Making gestures that congruently reflect your words and meaning will always enhance the impact of your voice.

Going over the top

Some people object that the air sculpture exercise makes them feel as if their behaviour while presenting is over the top, but invariably their listeners report a perfectly pitched presentation. When the session is played back on video, the presenter is usually pleasantly surprised. The few occasions when a presenter truly goes over the top are still useful as it stretches their boundaries and makes available a much wider area of middle-ground choices.

Air sculptures and voice work connect you more fully with your audience. You speak to their mind with your words while your posture and gestures paint compelling images in the space that hovers between presenter and audience.

Practical Exercise – Air Sculptures

1. The next time you see someone asking a local person for directions, watch how centred and attentive the local person is to the newcomer. Notice how they indicate left, right and straight ahead. How do you know when they are describing a significant landmark? How expansive and clear are the gestures? Does the tone of voice vary with the gestures? Do they maintain eye contact and adjust the pace of their speech to match the assimilation speed of the newcomer?
2. Try giving clear, well-paced directions to an imaginary stranger. If it makes it easier you can first practise the visual, vocal and verbal aspects of the directions separately then combine them. Feel free to amplify the elements more than you normally would.
3. Now apply the same skills to a small chunk of your presentation and see the difference they make.

MOVING EFFECTIVELY ON STAGE

Many presenters have times when they have to speak and move simultaneously: moving from one side of the stage to another to spread your attention to different sections of a large audience or to reach different items of professional equipment.

It is quite appropriate for a presenter to continue talking to the audience as he or she moves from one location to the other. Many presenters' method of moving is, however, highly inappropriate. For example, turning to face the object that they are walking towards and presenting their side profile or, even worse, their back to the audience. There are many problems associated with this way of moving:

1. Maximum visual presence is associated with 'full frontal' posture. The side view is much less impactful for the audience.
2. If you fully face one side of the stage you will have fully turned your back to the opposite side of the audience.
3. If you face the back of the stage you will have literally and metaphorically turned your back on the audience.

The stage walk

The stage walk is an excellent way of avoiding movement problems. It comprises a series of sideways, cross-over steps which help you to keep more of the front of your body facing the auditorium. It will probably feel a bit unfamiliar and crab-like at first. With practice it becomes flowing and easy and ensures that you communicate with maximum visual, vocal and verbal impact.

Practical Exercise – The stage walk

1. Pause and centre yourself. Scan the room using your full peripheral vision.
2. Practise crossing from one side of a room to the other by crossing your left foot in front of your right foot.
3. Now try it with your right foot crossing in front of your left, with the left foot crossing behind the right, then with right behind left.
4. Now try using different combinations of the above steps.
5. Do the stage walk as you recite a piece of poetry or a nursery rhyme.

Presenters who habitually bump into the furniture will find that they will become much more confident and assured in their movement if they practise using their peripheral vision as they move.

Even with practice, you are unlikely to walk in an absolutely straight line from one side of the room to another. You are much more likely to walk in gently curving lines. When you are addressing a group of listeners you will be able to select a curving stage walk that will be most suitable for the seating arrangements of the particular venue in which you are working.
Master the art of walking backwards while continuing to face the audience.

Practical Exercise – Walking backwards

1. Arrange two or three pieces of furniture to represent pieces of equipment that you might have on stage while speaking.
2. Move to the front of the room, pause and centre yourself. Expand your field of peripheral vision.
3. Briefly glance over your shoulder at the equipment. Look forward again.
4. Gently walk backwards until you are standing beside the equipment.
5. Repeat this until it becomes easy and familiar.
6. Now try walking backwards while reciting some poetry or a nursery rhyme.
7. Rehearse the walk as part of your presentation, with a mental picture of the venue.

Case Study - The stage walk and adrenaline control
During one management training course I worked with a delegate who delivered a presentation on the subject of life insurance. He was wonderfully enthusiastic and excited about his subject. Unfortunately his enthusiasm resulted in him walking round in circles as he talked. The more enthusiastic he became, the faster he walked. Faster walking led to faster talking and he became very red in the face. His non-verbal behaviour was so powerful that it literally made some people dizzy. Very few people were able to keep track of what he was saying. There was so much adrenalin coursing around his system that he felt even tenser when asked to stand still while speaking.
Practising the flowing, gentle and predictable curve of the stage walk allowed him to channel his adrenaline without suppressing it. His face changed back to his normal colouring. The added eye contact with his listeners encouraged him to slow down his speech to an understandable pace. As he continued to practise, his movements became more precise and graceful. This not only made him calmer but also allowed the audience to share some of his enthusiasm for his subject.

SPATIAL MARKING AND ANCHORING

Spatial marking is a way of using non-verbal behaviour to increase audience understanding, comprehension and recall of the subject on which you are speaking.

One of the most common and simple methods of marking out points of information in space and time is to be found in the expression:

"In the first place..."

the speaker makes their first point

"...and in the second place..."

the speaker makes their second point

"...and thirdly and finally..."

The speaker will frequently extend their thumb for the first place, their index finger for the second place and their middle finger for the final point.

The origins of the expression 'In the first place…' stretch back to the days of classical Greek oratory. The oratory competitions required the speakers to deliver enormously long speeches from memory – too long for the average memory – so the orators had to use memory triggers. One section of their address would be practised and memorised in a certain place, for example by a fountain, the next section would be set to memory on the steps of the judicial buildings and the following section by the senate house. When the orator delivered their address, they would visualise each location and thus recall each section of their speech in turn. Over time, this process was accompanied by the expression 'In the first place...'. The repeated use of this expression caused it to become a memory and orientation trigger not only for the speakers but also for the listeners.

Timelines

People understand time as having a quality of direction. One commonly understood timeline flows from the back (past) to the front (future). Consider expressions such as "That's all behind me now", referring to a past event, or "I see a bright future ahead for this student", implying a forwards direction to future events.

Another frequently used timeline is one that runs from left (the past) to right (the future). An example of this is 'before and after' photographs in adverts. By marking out specific points in a line that runs from the audience's left to the audience's right you can emphasize important points non-verbally as well as verbally.

Practical Exercise - Timeline

Practise creating a left to right timeline with some material that you have to present.

1. Choose three main points that you would like to emphasise, or mark out the beginning, middle and end of your presentation.
2. Stand in the middle of an imaginary presentation space. Remember to pause and centre yourself.
3. Introduce yourself to the imaginary audience and then move to the:
   a) right of stage (audience left) for the first point, e.g. "A high-fibre diet is good for your health."
   b) centre stage for the following point, e.g. "Dietary fibre is found in fruit and vegetables."
   c) left of stage (audience right) for the final point, e.g. "Be healthy! Eat more fruit and vegetables!"
4. Practise going through the whole procedure more minimally by standing still and gesturing with your:
   d) right hand (audience left) for the first point
   e) both hands for the next point
   f) left hand for the final point.

Spatial marking in business

The regional director of a high street retail chain addresses a group of area managers on how the company has been developing up to the present day and its possible direction over the next ten years. He stands in the centre of the speaking area, introduces himself and welcomes the managers to his talk. He then moves

two paces to audience left,

"Today I will talk about where we have come from"

back to centre stage

"where the company is in today's marketplace"

two paces to audience right

"and finally I will talk about my vision for our future"

By doing this he has neatly structured his presentation both verbally and non-verbally He has used his stage walk so that his voice is clear and his visual presence is strong. While moving, he has visually swept

the room and addressed his first three remarks to 'allies' within the audience.
The director then returns to the centre of the room and pauses for a couple of seconds to clear the slate for the main body of his talk. He then delivers each section of his presentation from the appropriate point on the stage. Audience attention and comprehension is kept high as they know, unconsciously, exactly where they are in the presentation with each shift the director makes.
The director concludes his presentation by standing centre stage and marking out his three points with hand gestures and eye directions:

"And to conclude my presentation"

gestures with right hand to audience left
"this is where we have come from"
both hands gesture towards mid-line
"this is our position today"
left hand to audience right
"and a golden future lies ahead!"

Try working out spatial marking for your self with the following text from Sir Walter Scott. Place "Adversity" on the audiences left. "Belief" in the centre and "Consequences" on the audience's right. Also experiment with physically moving audience left for "Adversity" centre for "Belief" and audience right for "Consequences". Have fun!

'It's a matter of ABC: When we encounter ADVERSITY, we react by thinking about it. Our thoughts rapidly congeal into BELIEFS. These beliefs may become so habitual we don't even realize we have them unless we stop to focus on them. And they don't just sit there idly; they have CONSEQUENCES. The beliefs are the direct cause of what we feel and what we do next. They can spell the difference between dejection and giving up, on the one hand, and well-being and constructive action on the other. The first step is to see the connection between adversity, belief, and consequence. The second step is to see how the ABCs operate every day in your own life.'
Sir Walter Scott

THE POWER OF COMMUNICATION

'There has been an upturn of confidence in the markets.'
'You're on shaky ground there.'
'The speech struck a chord with the public.'
'I smell a rat.'
'Let me chew it over for a while.'
'Keep in touch.'
'It was a very touching gesture.'

Some recent research gave an account of how people responded to different words. For example, words with a more visual nature elicited more activity in the brain's visual cortex. Words with a more auditory character tended to elicit more activity in the parts of the brain that processed auditory information. It therefore makes sense to use as wide a range of sensory words as possible to pull in the majority of an average audience.

There is no such thing as a single sense thinker. Everyone uses a variety of senses. By using a variety of sensory words, it is possible not only to build rapport with more of the audience but also to gain a deeper, unconscious rapport with each individual.

1. Light up your own brain first. Use clear and motivating metaphors to achieve a sensorial association with your material. When you present, you will be brighter and firing on all cylinders.
2. Start with feeling (slower) words, then move to (faster) visual words.
3. There are times when audiences are more than fully engaged, such as meetings where people are upset and angry. The use of fewer sensory and more emotionally neutral words can be extremely useful to help to calm such an atmosphere but only if you have acknowledged how your audience is feeling, otherwise you run the risk of being perceived as cold and uncaring.

- Chapter Seven -

PRACTICALITIES

'Whenever you are asked if you can do a job, tell 'em, 'Certainly I can!' Then get busy and find out how to do it.'
Theodore Roosevelt

'Practice is the best of all instructors.' *Publius Syrus*

DEVELOPING 'NOUS'

The word 'nous' (rhymes with 'mouse') means a kind of inbuilt knowledge — an unconscious competence or know-how. The information in this chapter will help to get in touch with your nous — your native wisdom of presenting.

On a day-to-day basis, you can help develop your nous by making the most of every opportunity:

- Listen to presentations given by your colleagues and other presenters on the same and other subjects. They may have an interesting and refreshingly different slant on presenting the same material.
- Attend conferences in your own field or fields of interest. This will give you the opportunity to study other presentations and will keep you at the sharp edge of your professional skills.
- Keep up to speed by reading professional journals, magazines and websites. Read the newspapers and keep clippings of interesting and topical articles. Use a good search engine to locate web pages on your subject.
- Search the growing number of quote sites on the internet for punchy quotes.
- Consider speaking at conferences and writing articles on your field of interest. This keeps your presence in the minds of others. Also, there is nothing like being in the firing line to keep you on your professional toes!
- Learn from the people to whom you present — they are quite possibly the best teachers you will ever have.

PRESENTATION STYLES

In order to choose the right style that will fit both you and your audience, you will need to do your research and become familiar with the needs, preoccupation and expectations of your audience. Some of the categories below will help you to think through your presentation more thoroughly and tailor it to fit your audience more comfortably.

Formal or informal?

This is more a question of style than of content or structure. The informal style is closer in quality to a conversational feel. It is more likely to have questions and clarifications included in the body of the presentation. The formal presentation is closer in quality to a public speaking style. Formality implies roles, which can create more emotional distance. This distance is bridged by a larger-than-life performance style. Many gifted public speakers and presenters have mastered the more intimate informal style even in the most formal, structured settings while speaking to large audiences.

Large or small?

Larger presentations require greater elements of performance, entertainment and audience stimulation within them. Because they generally involve less audience interaction, they tend to be more structured and formal. The smaller presentation, even when formal, tends to be more conversational and in a lower key - you do not want to blast your audience against the wall with an overly powerful delivery.

Tell or sell?

Are you seeking simply to inform your audience or do you want to get them to buy into an idea?

An informative 'tell' presentation is based around conveying factual information, for example at annual general meetings or induction training.

A 'sell' presentation will tend to concentrate more on getting the board, the committee, the members, the staff or the audience to buy into an idea, a policy or a course of action. It could use fear and apprehension - the stick - to get people to avoid moving in a certain direction. Or, more constructively, it can use inspiration and excitement - the carrot - to get people to move positively in a certain direction.

Mixing sell and tell

While a treasurer's report (for example) may be predominantly factual and informative, it should still have some of the colour, verve and personal touch associated with 'sell' presentations. It usually benefits from some sell to finish off:

"The organization has done very badly this year. We really need to get our act together and increase profits" or *"What a fantastic year it has been. If we keep going this way, next year will be even better."*

Participative

The participative presentation is usually set up in the style of 'tell' - the presenter or facilitator will set out the goals and objectives to be achieved or the agenda to be followed. In this situation, the audience gets involved in the action. The topics are discussed in a more spontaneous fashion or in a more formal, ordered fashion with audience members airing their views in sequence. The presenter may summarise the topics at the end of the meeting and set out any conclusions the group has reached.

Coaching and training

These presentations are based around imparting skills to or drawing out skills from the audience and tend to be delivered to smaller audiences.

Usually the trainer will give a background or history to the skill being studied. The trainer will then do a demonstration (often with a member of the audience) of the first few steps of the skill to be acquired. Once the skill has been explained and demonstrated, the group will then practise the new skills individually or in smaller groups. The trainer will present to the individual or groups in a more instructive coaching style until the new skill begins to click. The whole group will then reconvene and the presenter will talk through and demonstrate a new layer of sub-skills. The demonstration will usually incorporate questions, queries and clarifications from the practice and coaching section. In this way, layer by layer, a new skill set is developed by the group.

At the end of the course - often at the end of each sub section - the trainer will summarise previous steps, draw conclusions and make recommendations for future practice.

Internal or external?

Presenting to an internal audience is a bit like interacting with your family. There may be politics involved. There will be those with whom you have closer alliances and those with whom friction occurs more readily. Internal audiences tend to be less formal but it is a good idea to anticipate the objections and support you reasonably expect to receive from various quarters. Although you have a role and job description within the organisation, people have personal responses to you.

When you are presenting externally, you are functioning as a representative of your organisation or a representative of the ideas, products and services that you are wishing to sell. You will be perceived relatively less personally and relatively more as the role you represent.

USE OF VISUAL AIDS

Often presenters think that an electronic presentation - the visual aids that they use - PowerPoint, the overhead projection, the slide show - and that their part in this presentation is simply to supply a voice-over to the visuals. Often the psychology behind this approach is based on fear and on wanting to hide away. Remember that the best visual aids you have are your own body language, composure and knowledge of the subject. So ask yourself "Is this visual aid really necessary? Would my presentation really suffer without it?" If you find yourself honestly answering "no" to this question then have the courage of your convictions and leave it out. If the answer is "yes", then read on. The section below will provide some valuable tips for the best possible use of visual aids.

Visibility and clarity

For something to be a visual aid rather than a visual hurdle you must ask yourself:

- Can my visual aid be seen easily and clearly from all parts of the room?
- Is it simple, spare and succinct?

Visual aid or handout?

Often a lot of material which is displayed on projectors - long quotes, complex graphs and figures - would be better given as a handout. Cut out or simplify what you put on the projector and tell your audience that you will be providing additional information in the form of a handout at the end of your presentation. Do not give handouts at the beginning… your audience are only human and many of them will read the handout rather than look at or listen to you.

Non-verbal relationship to visual aids

Look, point, look back and speak…

When speakers are using a visual aid there is a powerful tendency to look at it while speaking, rather than looking at the audience. Not only does this reduce the speaker's visual impact, it also reduces their audibility. In most cases, the speaker does not actually have to use the visual aid for their memory - it is to aid audience comprehension and recall.

So:

1. Pause silently and **look** at the visual aid.
2. **Point** at the section to which you are referring.

3. **Look back** to the audience, then
4. **Speak** to the audience.

You could extend this attitude to all of the procedures you carry out on stage. The simplest activity carried out in an uncoordinated way can induce discomfort in both audience and presenter. Communicate comfort and ease by practising writing on the flip-chart, changing slides and switching projectors on and off using mind and body co-ordination.

For presentations where the venue itself is supplying the equipment, phone or write beforehand to make sure that they have everything you will need. If possible, get there the day before to physically check for yourself and to rehearse.

Low-tech longevity - the perennial flipchart

Why has the flipchart - the lowest-tech of visual aids - remained popular for such a long time? For a start, it is low-tech and there is less likely to go wrong with it. Flipcharts can be prepared in advance or they can be used to facilitate the here-and-now process of a presentation or training session. As well as writing on the flipchart, you can draw illustrative diagrams and pictures.

If you prepare your flipcharts before you arrive at the venue, make sure you have a way of transporting them so that they arrive in pristine condition. If you roll them up, take something to keep them flat when they are rolled out again.

- Practise writing on a flipchart until it becomes as clear as (or better than) your normal writing.
- Practise drawing any graphs, illustrations or pictures on the flipchart. Prepare these drawings beforehand or get someone else with good graphic skills to prepare them for you.
- Check that your presentation venue has flipchart pens, flipchart paper and blu-tack available for you to use.
- Take a spare set of pens with you - even if the venue has them they may not be working properly.
- Use clearly visible colours - blacks, blues, darker reds and greens. Yellows and oranges can sometimes be difficult to read. Pinks can be distracting.
- For more formal presentations, leave a blank sheet of paper between each written one, as the writing from the previous

sheet tends to show through. This is less important for informal presentations, training sessions or meetings.

- Use both upper case and lower case - using upper case only can make it difficult to read.
- Underlining can be useful for headings and important points.
- Some flip-chart pens have bladed tips - the thick edge can give a bold effect.

Projectors

For more formal or larger presentations, a projector can be very useful. As well as being larger than a flipchart, the image position on the screen or wall can be adjusted to give maximum visibility for everyone present.

- Make sure that you have a spare bulb! This is the most common cause of mechanical failure of all projectors, ancient or modern.
- Know your machine. How long does it take to warm up? Can you operate it without fumbling about? What kind of screen does it need?
- Buy an extension lead. A purchase worth its weight in gold - projector leads are often short and power points are often in inconvenient places. The extension lead will give you more choices about setting up the presentation room for maximum comfort and effect.
- Buy a remote or a handheld mouse if you use a laptop. Using the touch pad or a mat-bound mouse will have you bobbing up and down during your presentation. This will muffle your visual and vocal impact. A remote or handheld mouse will free your eyes and voice to attend to the audience, and will allow you to move more freely as you talk.
- Buy a small but powerful pair of computer speakers. If you use sound, especially in larger spaces, they will give a much louder, fuller sound than the speakers on your laptop.
- Take a plain white bed sheet and drawing pins. They will serve as a screen if there is nothing else available.

Popular programs - go easy

Certain presentation programs have become a victim of their own popularity and overuse. Even when electronic presentations are done cleverly and potentially entertainingly, they lose the audience's attention because they have become used to them. When it comes to presentations, you can't beat human contact. Mix your slides judiciously with stories from your and others' personal experiences, use demonstrations and get your audience as active and involved as possible. Within this context your slides will make much more impact.

Preparing slides

A small critique of some presenters - they just love to cram their slides to bursting point. Let's not confuse quantity with quality.
Clear all the distraction off the slides and have either:

Three bullets down with five words across

• Blah Blah Blah Blah Blah
• Blah Blah Blah Blah Blah
• Blah Blah Blah Blah Blah

OR

Five bullets down with three words across

• Blah Blah Blah
• Blah Blah Blah
• Blah Blah Blah
• Blah Blah Blah
• Blah Blah Blah

Any more than that and the audience will be reading the slides rather than listening to you.

The T-shirt theory (less is more)

How many words can you get on a T-shirt and still make sure it is readable to a passer-by? Slides should be the same - visual, aesthetic and minimalist.

- Clear the clutter by removing company logos and repetitive headings from every slide - using them at the beginning and end will be quite sufficient.
- Use simple or familiar fonts that are easy to read:
- A sans serif font is easier to read than something fancy like *this*. Times New Roman is a familiar newspaper font. A mix of Upper Case and Lower Case is easier to read THAN

CONSTANT CAPITALS. Use **bold text** for added effect. Use italics and underlining sparingly.

- Add a bit of colour - but not so much that it becomes a distraction.
- Get sumone to check your speling for oblivious and sutble misteaks!
- Check your sequence once, twice and thrice.
- Check the sequence of acetates, slides or PowerPoint slides repeatedly. They have a mind of their own and like to come out at night and swap places.
- Make sure that computer presentations are backed up on a 'cloud' type account (Dropbox, Googledrive, or similar) or on CD, USB stick, etc. Computer gremlins have a wicked sense of humour and will save the most serious technical hitches for the most inconvenient and embarrassing moments. Post your most important files to yourself at a web-based email address so that they will be ready to download at your convenience anywhere that you have an internet connection.

MICROPHONES AND PA SYSTEMS

Avoid using amplification except when absolutely necessary. Use the voice exercises in Chapter 6 to enhance your audibility instead. The checklist for when you are considering whether amplification is required is as follows:

- The types of situation where you may need to use a microphone are at conferences or large public meetings. The acoustics vary tremendously, so get there early and do an audibility check with a friend or colleague.
- A cordless collar microphone is preferable to a fixed microphone and will allow you to move around.
- If you have never heard your voice amplified before, it can be a bit of a shock. Rehearse thoroughly with a microphone.
- If you have to use a fixed microphone, adjust it upwards or downwards until it is about six inches away from your mouth. Avoid pushing your mouth any closer to the microphone. It is particularly important to do a comparative sound check in situations where one presenter follows another — especially if the previous speaker has a much louder or softer voice than you.
- Public address systems have a tendency to make odd noises or to cut out. Check the equipment and, if necessary, make sure it is fixed in time for your presentation.

PREPARING THE ROOM

This section assumes that you have a reasonable degree of control over the environment in which you will be presenting. It ends by making a few suggestions about what to do if you have a potentially poor environment. Get to your venue in advance and check it thoroughly.

Accessibility

This is an extremely important factor if you are booking and organizing the event yourself. Consider public transport links, car parking and access for people with disabilities. For longer events you should also consider the local availability of decent overnight accommodation that will suit all budgets.

Room availability

Check beforehand that the room is actually available. If possible, get a written acknowledgement of this. Do you need break-out rooms for certain sessions? Check that they are also available and booked.

Room size

Is the room large enough for the expected size of audience? Will they be packed in like sardines or feel dwarfed and alienated by the size of the venue? Try to get the right balance between the anticipated size of your audience and the room available.

Seating arrangements and furniture

Appropriate comfort is again the key. Look for upright chairs with shoulder and leg room.

For larger audiences, theatre-style rows are the most convenient method of seating. For audiences of twenty and under, consider a horseshoe arrangement of chairs.

Unless there is a lot of writing or note taking to be done, avoid having tables in front of the audience's chairs or your chair, as they get in the way of activities you may have planned and create an emotional barrier between presenter and audience.

For audiences of up to one hundred and where there is a fair amount of individual, partner or small group activity involved, consider presenting in the round for some of the time. Start off with the audience seated theatre style. When it comes to break-out time, ask them to move their chairs to the edge of the room to create more space - a wonderful way to get audience activity and participation started. When you come back to whole group activity, you can present from the middle of the room. Your voice and body language will need to be sufficiently strong to deal with this. If you are using your voice effectively, you should be just as audible to the people behind you as to those in front and to the sides of you. You will, however, need to rotate slowly, like the beam from a lighthouse, to give everyone sufficient visual contact with you. You also have the option of standing, along with everyone else, at the perimeter of the circle and presenting from there.

For participatory, training and celebratory events, presenting in the round is one of the most powerful tools for dissolving the barriers between presenter and audience.

For smaller meetings, the round table (although not always readily available) is much less confrontational in style than square or rectangular tables. Given that round tables are not that common, get to the meeting early enough to get the seat of your choice - maximum visibility and audibility.

Lighting

Know where the light switches are! There will usually be more than one light in each room. Switch them on and off. Keep experimenting and adjusting until you get the most consistent spread of light. Windowless rooms, or rooms with fluorescent lighting, sap energy and consequently audience attention spans. Wherever possible, give your presentations in a room with windows and good natural lighting, or with non-fluorescent light sources.

Go and sit where the audience will be sitting and check that there will be no glaring lights shining into their eyes from where you, the presenter, will be standing. Avoid standing or sitting with your back to a window - especially when the sun is shining directly through it and into the eyes of the audience.

Acoustics

Some environments seem to absorb sound like a sponge - there are often lots of soft furnishings, thick carpets and curtains in these settings. Other environments reflect and echo sound more readily - often places with a lot of hard surroundings (concrete, glass, metal) and they can become noisy too easily.

Get to your venue early and do a sound check, whether you are being amplified or not. If your voice needs more power, do not simply try to speak louder. Centre yourself and imagine that you are singing as you

speak. In addition to bringing out more dynamic variation in your voice, this will also bring out some of the higher, more carrying frequencies. A small stage - as little as 30 cm higher than floor level - can make the world of difference to your audibility.
Make eye contact! If you can focus on your audience, they will probably hear you.

Atmosphere, ventilation and temperature
Air is brain fuel, so make sure there is sufficient ventilation. Familiarise yourself with the heating and air conditioning systems in the room. Be prepared to use the doors and windows judiciously. Check verbally with your audience by asking if the temperature is suitable - and non-verbally - i.e. are they drooping, nodding off, fanning themselves, shivering? If in doubt, go for a slightly cooler atmosphere and keep them warm and attentive by having activity and audience participation breaks more often.
Harsh or tedious environments can be softened or enlivened with flowers, plants and topic-related posters.

Refreshments
Coffee and tea are commonly supplied as refreshments in business environments. Herbal teas and bottled water are becoming increasingly available. Of all the drinks available, water is absolutely the most essential brain fuel available: it aids thinking, concentration and intellectual ability. Consider also adding fresh fruit to your afternoon and morning breaks, as well as biscuits.

Toilet facilities
It doesn't matter how good a presenter you are... you simply cannot compete with that kind of discomfort. Make sure that toilet facilities are available nearby!

- Chapter Eight -

FEEDBACK

'Learning is not compulsory — neither is survival.'
W. Edwards Demming

'The meaning of your communication is the response you get. Keep adjusting your communication until you get the response that you desire.'
John Grinder and Richard Bandler

HOW DID YOU DO?

You know your material inside out, back to front, left, right and centre. This gives you the control that allows you to track and read the audience. You can afford to deconstruct and reconstruct your presentation for them as you go along.

Before you reach this level of simultaneous output and feedback, you will need to spend time on a more sequential mode of feedback - you do your presentation then you receive feedback from various sources. From this feedback, you should take notice of the areas where you need further development and work, and acknowledge and reinforce your areas of excellence and strength. Rehearse your chosen areas for development and implement these improvements in future presentations.

Nowadays many businesses use some type of questionnaire to elicit specific feedback from clients, customers or audience. Think of the places where you have seen them — hotels, restaurants, conferences, training sessions and so on. The forms are usually split into several categories which, added together, give full and complete feedback on the session or service being provided. Each category is scored for quality or satisfaction. For example:

Excellent Good Average Poor Very poor

Other possibilities are a percentage for each category, with 100 per cent being equivalent to the peak of excellence and zero per cent equivalent to poorest of the poor. If you intend to become a great presenter, you should be aiming to consistently score 85 per cent and above, or for most of your scores to be in the ‘excellent’ category. Who is it that decides what is good or poor when you are giving a presentation? The audience does. And so do you. It is also extremely helpful to have a close but objective friend or colleague to be present as an observer at your presentations. This will take care of feedback from first, second and third positions.

Case Study – Dr Brent Young
Dr Brent Young, professor at the Imperial College of Science, Technology and Medicine, noticed a pattern of feedback emerging. Out of a class of students, he consistently found that while the vast majority of the class scored him highly, by the end of the academic year two or three students would assess him poorly.
He dealt with this in the first class of the year by telling the students that in the assessments at the end of the academic year he was highly rated by 97 per cent of his students. He then went on to say *"and for the two or three of you here who are going to think that I am a complete _____, I apologise in advance!"*
He set the expectations for learning and fun high, and was also gracious enough to let people dislike him.

Evolving your own feedback form
Below is a sample feedback form that you could use or adapt for your own purposes and circumstances:

How would you rate the presentation overall?
Excellent □ **Good** □ **Average** □ **Poor** □ **Very poor** □
What points worked well? What needs developing?

How would you rate the presenter's body language?
Excellent □ **Good** □ **Average** □ **Poor** □ **Very poor** □
What points worked well? What needs developing?

How would you rate the presenter's use of the voice?
Excellent □ **Good** □ **Average** □ **Poor** □ **Very poor** □
What points worked well? What needs developing?

How would you rate the content and structure of the presentation?
Excellent □ **Good** □ **Average** □ **Poor** □ **Very poor** □
What points worked well? What needs developing?

How would you rate the use of audio-visuals?
Excellent □ **Good** □ **Average** □ **Poor** □ **Very poor** □
What points worked well? What needs developing?

How emotionally committed to his/her subject did the presenter seem to be?

Comments:

- Chapter Nine -

BALANCING WORK WITH THE REST OF YOUR LIFE

'... bump, bump, bump, on the back of the head, behind Christopher Robin. It is, as far as he knows, the only way of coming downstairs, but sometimes he feels that there really is another way, if only he could stop bumping for a moment and think of it.'
A.A. Milne, Winnie The Pooh

Rhythm and the art of management maintenance

There is an old Japanese Zen story in which the master is asked the secret of his enlightenment. *'When I am hungry I eat. When I am tired I sleep,'* the master enigmatically replies.

'How ordinary!' you may be thinking. But think a bit longer. Who in the world of business do you know who can put their feet up when they feel the need? At the very least it requires an office with a lock on the door and perhaps someone to hold all calls. There are the lucky few in upper management or those who work from home who can do this. Those who do, swear that it profoundly enhances their alertness, productivity and creativity.

Compare this to the energy cycles of an ordinary office. One moment, you're bright-eyed and bushy-tailed. Ten minutes later, tempers are fraying with colleagues and customers, silly mistakes are made on the computer, coffee cups are tipped over documents and personal memory banks short circuit for no apparent reason. What causes these phenomena that do so much to interfere with a company's competitiveness?

Everyone is aware of the 24-hour rhythm of sleeping and waking. There are also other, shorter, rhythms of drowsiness and alertness which last from 90 minutes to two hours, known as Ultradian Rhythms. Most people are vaguely aware of this shorter rhythm, one famous example being the conference mid- afternoon graveyard shift which is dreaded by so many.

Research into the body's Ultradian Rhythms started in the 1950s. The researchers found that the Ultradian Rhythms affected both mental and physical performance — concentration, memory, learning, creativity, physical co-ordination, reflexes and energy levels. It was also established that long-term interference with these rhythms was associated with a host of stress-related conditions that led to mediocre performance.

These rhythms are unconsciously recognised in the way that a standard working day is organised, for example with tea breaks in the mid-morning and mid-afternoon. This has traditionally given employees a vitally needed break in which they can refresh and rejuvenate both mind and body. However, many companies have slimmed down the size of their workforce with the result that a single employee may be doing a job that was previously covered by two or even three people.

This leads to situations where employees, through a sense of guilt, fear or duty, regularly override their natural rhythms - breaks are skipped and with them the opportunity to follow the natural drowsy and rejuvenating aspect of the Ultradian cycle.

Rest and replenishment

Typically the resting part of the daily cycle either escapes our notice or is ignored. Stimulants such as sugary snacks, coffee or simply gritting the teeth are used to override our needs for rest and replenishment and this sends us into adrenaline overdrive. These addictive habits eventually catch up with people through health problems and/or errors in judgement.

So what are the signs and signals that can alert you to the need for an 'energy exchange'? Yawning, drowsiness, mind wandering, dreaminess, irritability, muscular tension, muscular slackness and even the need for the toilet are all signs that you are approaching the energy trough. In the best of all possible worlds, you would then lie down for 20 minutes, focus on the most comfortable part of your body and let the comfort spread. But not everybody works in a sympathetic context where it is possible to take a 20 minute break. Some people will lock themselves in the toilet for five minutes and let their mind wander, others may go for walk around the block or the building, or simply stand up for a stretch and a yawn. In all these cases, there is a shift down in gear from a goal-getting pace to a less hurried, process orientated pace. It is at this point of detachment from the goal orientated tasks that many people find the creative solution to problems.

This is a more naturalistic approach to stress management that, with a little practice, anybody can incorporate into the midst of their working life.

Timing critical appointments

So how can you organize yourself and your staff so that you are winners in the marketplace and deliver great presentations?

1. Companies will get their money's worth from an employee who takes breaks - respect individual working rhythms as the foundations of high performance.
2. Take breaks during meetings and presentations when significant numbers of people show signs of going into energy troughs.

Encourage 'spacing out' (dreaming) during breaks as a way of generating high-quality solutions to problems.
3. Wherever possible, schedule important meetings, phone calls, presentations and negotiations to coincide with high-performance energy peaks.

Case Study - Robin Prior

"One of the ways I've put life balance across to people is through the analogy of the milking stool. The milking stool has three legs and they represent, in your life, the work that you do, your home and love life, and your hobbies and pastimes. These three legs need to be well in place in order to have a balanced life.

Many people try to balance on one leg alone. There are many people who put all their time, energy and attention into their jobs. And then they wonder why the rest of their life doesn't work. And they also wonder why, overall, they are not happy.

There is this work ethic, a whole fallacy around commitment to a job, that unless you are giving everything of your self to the job, you are not doing it properly. In fact the evidence seems to be very clear now — if you just do a sensible number of hours, with a sensible level of commitment, you live a balanced life and actually do a better job.

What seems to happen is that when you restrict the number of hours that people work, they use their ingenuity to find simpler ways of doing what needs to be done. They do as much but in less time, and with less negative impact on the rest of their life."

- Chapter Ten -

ALEXANDER TECHNIQUE HISTORY & BACKGROUND

'Everything should be made as simple as possible, but no simpler.'
Albert Einstein

'It has helped me to undo knots, unblock energy and deal with almost paralysing stage fright'
William Hurt, actor from STAT website

'I find the Alexander Technique very helpful in my work. Things happen without you trying. They get to be light and relaxed. You must get an Alexander teacher to show it to you.'
John Cleese

What is the Alexander Technique?

Thirty years ago, when I qualified as an Alexander Technique teacher, there was nothing I hated more than being at a social event and someone asking me "What is the Alexander Technique?"

I'd launch into something like this:

"The Alexander Technique teacher uses their hands to lengthen your spine; they coax you into moving lightly and easily; this induces a sense of calm and well being; the teacher accompanies these wonderful experiences with careful verbal directions!"

The hapless questioner would look longingly across the room for more mainstream company…

It's easier now. Many more people have heard about the Alexander Technique, specifically in relation to back pain and posture, since it was recognised by the National Institute for Clinical Excellence (NICE).

Nowadays, when someone asks "What is the Alexander Technique?" I'm much more likely to respond with something basic like *"People find it really useful for dealing with bad backs, stiff necks and assorted stresses and strains." or "Actors and singers find that it frees their voice and reduces stage fright."*

Mostly this just leads on to general conversation like *"Have you worked with anyone famous?"* At which point I look knowing and smug and reply *"Oh I couldn't possibly say. Confidentiality and all that!"*

If the questioner is genuinely curious and asks *"OK but how, exactly, does it help back backs; free the voice; reduce stress?"* I will then probably give them a potted history of F.M. Alexander and his discoveries.

The Alexander Story

Frederick Matthias Alexander (1869 – 1955) was an actor who suffered from career threatening vocal and breathing difficulties. He specialised in a one-man show, in large provincial theatres, requiring a spirited and powerful delivery. A popular actor, Alexander could be on stage six evenings per week plus several matinees. This took its toll in the form of hoarseness, an audible rasping inhalation between phrases and an inflammation of his throat. The whole symptom picture was known as 'clergyman's sore throat'.

Medical interventions were largely fruitless, so Alexander pursued his own approach. He concluded that his symptoms were less to do with over-use and more a case of misuse. Alexander embarked on a painstaking period of self observation stretching out over several years. To aid his self-study Alexander set up a three-way system of mirrors in which could observe himself while reciting.

As a result of this self observation Alexander realised that he was, unconsciously, throwing a spanner in his own works. Through observation and reasoning he stopped sabotaging his own efforts and consequently freed up the functioning of his voice, breathing and general well-being. I will describe this in fuller detail in the following section.

Alexander was able to return to the stage. Soon after this he was inundated with actors and singers wanting lessons in his method. Alexander found it difficult to pass on his insights verbally. He developed a method of gentle manual guidance and verbal coaching and gave his pupils an experience of using their voice in an easier, more efficient and poised way.

It became clear to Alexander that his approach could have a beneficial effect not just on the voice but on all-round functioning and well being.

Into the Looking Glass

"Breathing, standing, walking and sitting, although innate, along with our growth, are apt, as movements, to suffer from defects in our ways of doing them... The faults tend to escape our direct observation and recognition... To watch another performer trying the movement can be helpful; or a looking-glass in which to watch ourselves trying it. The mirror can often tell us more than the most painstaking attempt to introspect" Sir Charles Sherrington - Nobel Prize for medicine

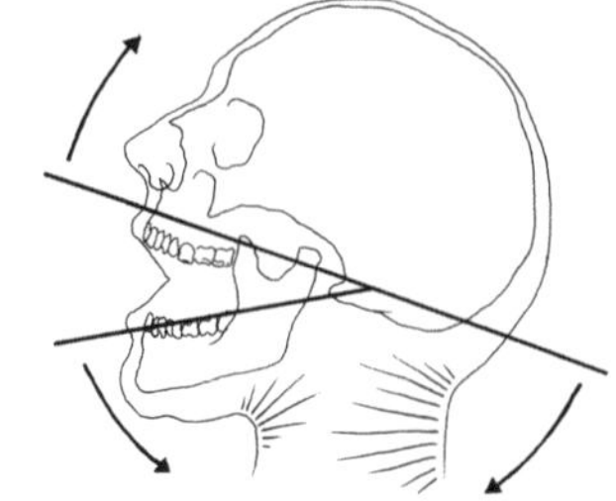

As he gazed into his mirrors Alexander noticed nothing unusual in his manner of reciting – in the first instance. Gradually he became aware of a tendency to stiffen his neck, pull his head back and compress his larynx when he anticipated reciting a difficult passage. This pattern was associated

with effortful inhalation. If the initial contraction was strong enough it could affect the whole balance of his system from head to toe.
From these initial observations Alexander brought about a complete change in his way of breathing, using his voice and in his general day to day functioning. It wasn't all plain sailing – there were several blind alleys.

The Principles

The method he settled on revolved around three main principles:

Direction
Sensory Appreciation
Pausing

Direction

Alexander noticed that pulling his head back and down was linked with his voice problems. So he tried physically moving the position of his head - putting it 'forwards and upwards' via direct muscular effort. This didn't help. The mirrors showed that instead of putting his head forwards and upwards he was either pulling it back and down, as before, or that he was pulling his head forwards and downwards – a different kind of badly.

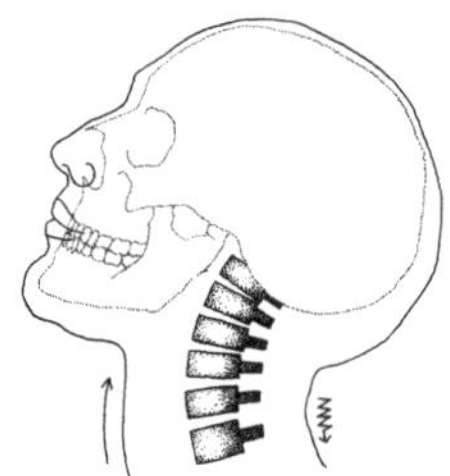

Back & down

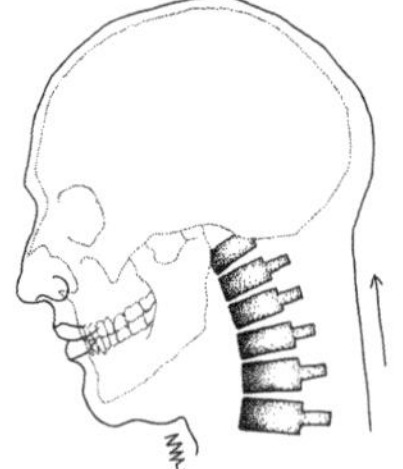

Forward & down

It became clear that there was a gulf between what he felt he was doing and what the mirrors reflected back to him. To use Alexander's terminology – his 'sensory appreciation' was unreliable.
Pre-school children, unconsciously, have this quality that Alexander teachers' call 'direction'. Easy, upright and poised in stillness and activity.

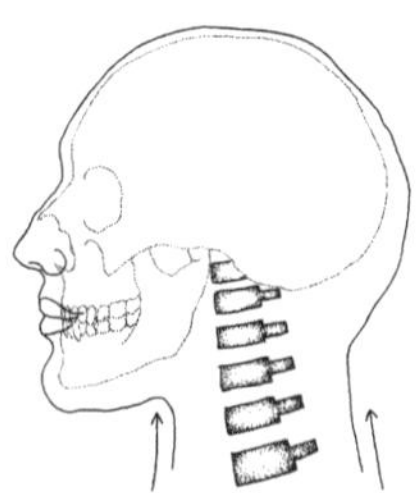

Forwards & upwards

As adults we can consciously develop ease and poise in our daily activities. It doesn't come from exhortations to "Sit up straight!" or "Stand up straight!" and the increasing strain and, eventually, deeper slumping that this causes.

Alexander formulated a series of what he called his 'directions' which took care of the critical relationship between the neck, head and torso. Alexander repeated the directions silently to himself:

Neck to be free
Head to go forwards and upwards
Back to lengthen and widen.

He 'projected' these directions without trying to physically impose them and without even caring whether they took seed or not. Gradually his mirrors demonstrated that the directions were beginning to take seed and slowly grow spreading through his entire frame.

Sensory Appreciation

Alexander realised that his habits (neck stiffening, pulling his head back and down, shortening and narrowing his back) felt, if not exactly right, then at least so overwhelmingly familiar that he tended to revert to them at the critical moment of actually reciting. Change doesn't always feel right. What we sense physically can be unreliable.

A little girl with an extremely twisted stance was brought to see Alexander. Alexander, using his expert touch, gently brought her into relative balance and symmetry. The result? She complained to her mother "The nasty man's twisted me all up!"

We all need a little time and tolerance to get used to new, unfamiliar, but ultimately healthier conditions.

Pausing

When Alexander eventually noticed his habit – neck stiffening, pulling his head back, shortening his spine and narrowing his back – he wasn't surprised that it took him so long to observe them. They were small, subtle habits. Tiny tensions. Like water dripping onto granite, year after year, and gradually changing its shape, we don't notice the build-up of misdirection through our system, until the pain or stress makes us take notice. And even then we only notice the effects, not the causes.

Alexander continually brought himself up to the point of reciting. Up to the point of almost stiffening his neck and pulling his head back. And then, so to speak, he would step back, be still and refresh his directions, "Neck... head... back."

And so Alexander navigated himself into that little known area that lies between stimulus and response. He found that he was able to maintain a more poised use of himself whilst reciting. He recited without stiffening his neck, pulling his head back and down and without shortening and narrowing his back. The results were from hoarseness to vocal clarity, from audibly rasping his breath in to smooth, quiet, efficient breathing - minimum effort and maximum effect.

And so he returned to the stage, briefly, before embarking on a career of teaching what he called "The Work". Until his death in 1955, he continually developed this method of gentle manual guidance and verbal coaching and gave his pupils a way to improve their functioning throughout the range of their day to day activities. "The Work" brought him to London in 1904 where he taught the top people from theatre and the arts. People from all walks of life (including politics, science, medicine, the aristocracy) were drawn to the work which made such a significant difference, mentally and physically, to their daily lives.

Alexander used observation and reasoning and through this gained a new experience of using himself in daily life. We tend to do it the other way round. We get an experience directly from the hands of an Alexander Technique teacher and understanding slowly follows.

Lesson Description

So what does a contemporary Alexander Technique lesson actually look like and sound like?

It can be difficult to describe an activity that has such a large sensory component. Here are some photos, with comments, so you can at least

get a fly on the wall perspective of what a typical Alexander Technique lesson might look like.
The upright work focuses on activities such as:

- Standing
- sitting
- walking
- bending
- breathing
- speaking
- using the arm and hands.

These activities work beautifully within the relatively small working space of most Alexander Technique teaching studios – they are also at the core of daily life for most people.
As a general rule, Alexander Technique teachers tend to work from the core of the body - neck, head and back - out towards the extremities, i.e. the arms and legs. They will also tend to divide the session into two phases - upright work and semi-supine with the pupil lying on a comfortably firm couch.
The upright work will usually consist of activities like standing, sitting, bending, walking and breathing.
The work in the semi-supine position reinforces the expansion throughout the core of the body – neck, head and back. It also allows an opportunity for exploring a more sensitive use of the arms and legs via passive, teacher guided movement.

"Allow your neck to be free"

"… so that your head can go forwards & upwards"

"…allowing your back to lengthen & widen"

"...allow your knees to go forwards and apart."

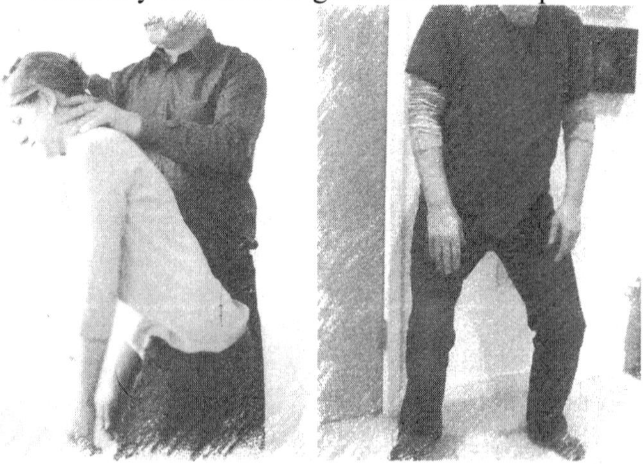

In practice, most Alexander Technique teachers do not recite the directions parrot-fashion. The words and language tend to be naturalistic and tailored to fit the individual.

Arms & Legs - Although there are specific directions for the arms & legs often the teacher will ask the pupil to continue focussing on their neck, head and back relationship as they work with the arms and the legs.

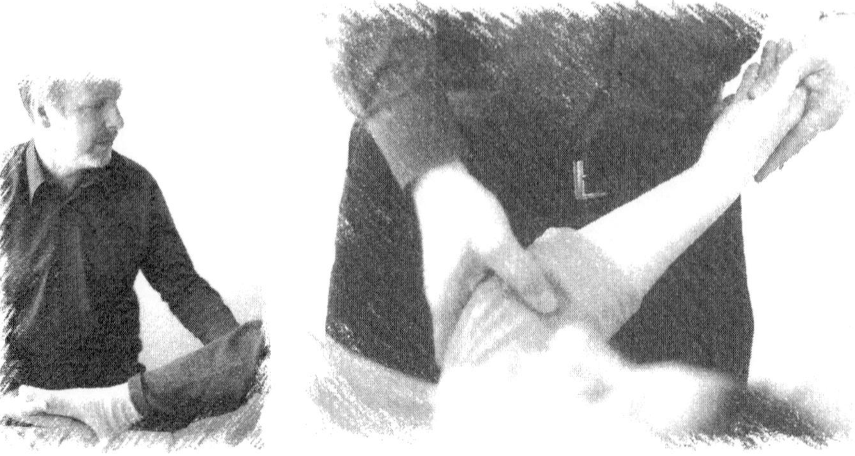

The major muscles that move the limbs have their origins in the torso. So working with the neck, head back relationship automatically influences the movement of the arms and legs.

The converse is also true – working with the arms and legs will reinforce release and expansion through the neck, head and back.

Application Technique

I was fortunate to be trained as an Alexander Technique teacher by Paul Collins - Canadian marathon gold medallist, principal orchestral violinist, Director of Alexander Technique teacher training, veterans' super-distance running world title holder.

Alexander teachers frequently abbreviate the term 'Alexander Technique' to 'AT'. Paul Collins used to insist (slightly tongue in cheek) that 'AT' should more correctly be 'Application Technique'. This was very much reflected in his approach to training teachers where we applied Alexander Technique to singing, running, playing an instrument, mind-mapping, etc.

Nowadays it is possible to attend a wide variety of courses that feature the 'Application Technique' - Alexander Technique is applied to swimming, running, singing, dancing, public speaking, acting, horse riding, playing musical instruments, martial arts etc.

For many years, I specialised in teaching Alexander applied to the Japanese martial art Aikido. The small female student in the pictures below is applying the principle of 'minimum effort maximum effect' (a principle common to both philosophies) to diffuse my 15 stone attack. I am using the same principles to land on the ground safely. After which I returned to my feet, dusted myself off, ready to deal with the next engagement!

And that, I believe, is the main reason why people keep coming back to the Alexander Technique – it is extremely calming and centring. It's not just a great way of adjusting posture. It is a psycho-physical technique that encourages increasing resourcefulness, poise, resilience and cheerfulness in dealing with the events of daily life.

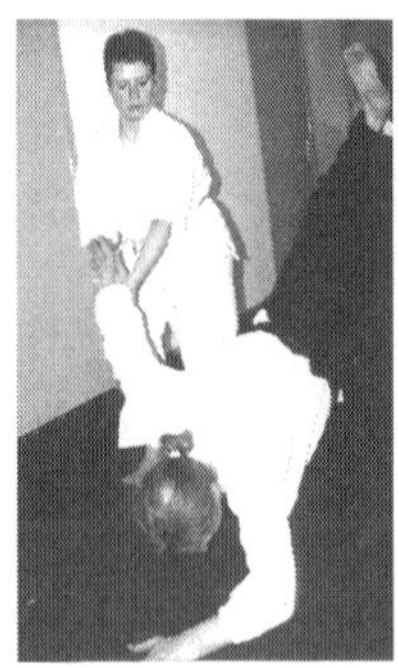

- Chapter Eleven -

THE SEMI-SUPINE ACTIVE RESTING POSITION

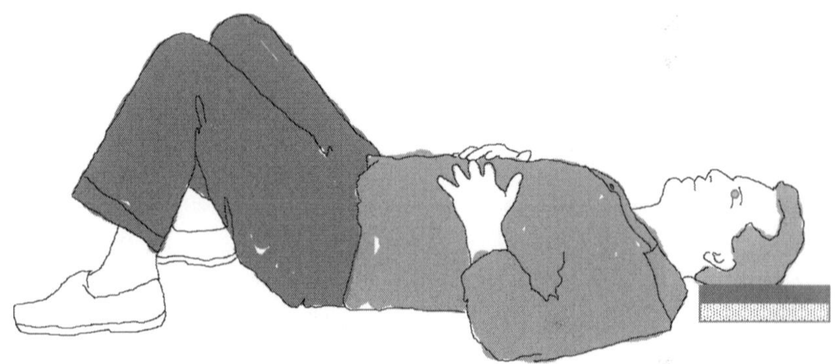

SEMI-SUPINE POSITION BENEFITS

The semi-supine active resting position is a procedure that I positively encouraged my drama students to do on a daily basis. It's simple and yields benefits out of proportion to the effort that one puts in. It is particularly calming and centring. It reinforces open and confident body language. It's the ideal pre-cursor to voice-work. No wonder my students continue to practice it decades after being introduced to it! The semi-supine position gives optimum support to your spine in particular; to your torso as a whole; it reduces pressure on the inter-vertebral discs; and it creates vocal freedom by encouraging your torso to unwind, lengthen and widen.

Preparation

- Time required 5 – 15 minutes
- Loosen tight clothing- and remove shoes.
- Gather several slim paperback books to use as a headrest.
- Find space on a warm carpeted floor on which to lie down.

Semi-Supine Position Equipment

- Use a firm and warm surface, such as a blanket on the floor.
- Place 1-3 inches of paperback books under the back of your skull to serve as a headrest.
- The headrest helps release the muscles that join the top of your spine to the base of your skull. The headrest should be neither too high (your chin will compress your throat) nor too low (your chin will stick up in the air).
- Place your feet flat on the floor, about shoulder-width apart, with your knees pointing up to the ceiling.
- Rest your hands, palms down, on your torso.

Getting Into the Semi Supine Position

Look at the diagram on the next page several times to get a general idea of how to get into (and out of) the semi-supine position. The sequence may seem long – but in practice it becomes very fluid. Move into the semi-supine position mindfully, quite slowly and with awareness. The same goes for returning to your feet again.

Bullet point Alexander directions
Over the next 5 – 20 minutes you will develop your relationship with the floor, and headrest, underneath you…

Imagine the four 'corners' of your back (head, shoulders and tail bone) spreading, lengthening and widening away from each other and on to the floor...

Let it be effortless. Leave it to gravity, the support under you and muscular release.

Sensing the support underneath you…

under your feet, your arms, your hands...
the headrest underneath your head…
the support under the length and width of your back...

With one big, broad, easy sweep, spread your attention to encompass

your whole body...
from top to bottom...
from side to side…

Continue sensing the support as you spread your attention to encompass your whole body.

Thinking of your whole back spreading and lengthening and widening onto the support underneath you...
your head releasing away from your tail bone…
as your tail bone also releases away from your head...
your whole back widening onto the floor.

Thinking of widening across your shoulders...

observing the length from your shoulders to your elbows...
observing the length from your elbows to your wrists...
and from your wrists to your fingertips.

Returning to your back – lengthening and widening and spreading...

finally thinking of your knees releasing up to the ceiling...

as your feet spread, lengthening and widening, onto the floor.

And, when you are ready, slowly and mindfully return to standing… Slowly, easily, with awareness.

Simply enjoy standing still for a moment - being on the ground, effortlessly occupying your full length and width.

Quietly, receptively, be aware of what you hear and see around you.

- Chapter Twelve -

THE PRACTISED PAUSE

'The most precious things in speech are pauses.'
Sir Ralph Richardson – Actor. 1902 – 1983

'I don't think I handle the notes much differently from other pianists. But the pauses between the notes - ah, there is where the artistry lies!'
Artur Schnabel - Musician1882 - 1951

SILENCE, PAUSING AND PUNCTUATION

Punctuation started appearing in Greek theatre about 2500 years ago. Punctuation marks gave the actor an indication of where to breathe and of how long to pause to give the written passage proper expression. Over the ensuing centuries this developed into something of a science with different punctuation marks indicating shorter or longer pauses. Today we tend to assume the written word will be read silently - for much of history it was assumed that the written word would be spoken publicly. During the English Civil War, there was an explosion of publishing, with each side busily printing its own publicity and propaganda. Only about 10% of the population was literate but everybody needed to know what was happening in their world. If you were literate, you were a presenter - the chances were that you would be required to read out the news to everyone else in the community.

'The right word may be effective, but no word was ever as effective as a rightly timed pause.' Mark Twain 1835-1910

Let's explore this by reciting 14 lines of Shakespeare – the master of the written word translated to speech...

Sonnet 18

Shall I compare thee to a summer's day?
Thou art more lovely and more temperate:
Rough winds do shake the darling buds of May,
And summer's lease hath all too short a date:
Sometime too hot the eye of heaven shines,
And often is his gold complexion dimm'd;
And every fair from fair sometime declines,
By chance or nature's changing course untrimm'd;
But thy eternal summer shall not fade
Nor lose possession of that fair thou owest;
Nor shall Death brag thou wander'st in his shade,
When in eternal lines to time thou growest:
So long as men can breathe or eyes can see,
So long lives this and this gives life to thee.

I'm indebted to actor and colleague Alison Skilbeck for introducing me to this exercise.

Every line has ten syllables and every line, apart from line 9, has a punctuation mark. One of the original functions of a punctuation mark was an instruction to breathe. The pattern of ten syllables and a punctuation mark is an easy, regular rate for the speaker. The regular pauses give the listener plenty of opportunity to assimilate the speaker's message. Not only is it a calming and centring pace for the speaker - it is also calming and centring for the listener. It's the closest thing to BBC newsreader rate of speech that I know of – the most widely comprehended and authoritative delivery of English on the globe.

Try doing the sonnet with some deliberate pausing at the beginning, end and between each phrase.

The symbol / represents a click of your fingers; or a gentle clap of your hands; or patting your thigh with your hand.

/// Shall I compare thee to a summer's day? //
Thou art more lovely and more temperate: //
Rough winds do shake the darling buds of May, //
And summer's lease hath all too short a date: //
Sometime too hot the eye of heaven shines, //
And often is his gold complexion dimm'd; //
And every fair from fair sometime declines, //
By chance or nature's changing course untrimm'd; //
But thy eternal summer shall not fade //
Nor lose possession of that fair thou owest; //
Nor shall Death brag thou wander'st in his shade, //
When in eternal lines to time thou growest: //
So long as men can breathe or eyes can see, //
So long lives this and this gives life to thee. ///

With mindful repetition and practice you can internalise this sense of stillness and pausing between the phrases. With further practice the pause transforms from a skilful behaviour and becomes an increasingly embedded attitude.

Who are you speaking to?

Here is a modern English translation of Sonnet 18. It's not scholarly and really doesn't have the poetry of the original but if you read it through a few times it will help to bring the original to life. It's an expression of love. Imagine that you are lovingly 'speaking to' someone rather than "talking at" an audience!

Shall I compare you to a summer's day?
You are more lovely and more constant:
Rough winds shake the beloved buds of May
And summer is far too short:
At times the sun is too hot,
Or often goes behind the clouds;
And everything beautiful sometime will lose its beauty,
By misfortune or by nature's planned out course.
But your youth shall not fade,
Nor will you lose the beauty that you possess;
Nor will death claim you for his own,
Because in my eternal verse you will live forever.
So long as there are people on this earth,
So long will this poem live on, making you immortal.

Practice Pausing...

'Don't just do something, stand there!'
Attributed to many, including the White Rabbit

'I like to talk about a thing I call a "practiced pause."
Just a few moments of pausing allows me
to consider a circumstance and take stock
of what the best direction might be.
Reactions tend to rise from habit and unconsidered action.
A Response is considered and thoughtful'.
Mary Anne Radmacher

'One choice is no choice at all. Two choices is a dilemma. Only when you get to three choices can you really be said to have truly said to have choice.'
Attributed to many

The techniques in this book can be transferred from presentation and performance skills to any sphere of daily life. The conscious pause is a powerful way of unhooking yourself from the restrictions of habitual reaction. Our habitual reactions are usually so well practised that they feel familiar and natural despite the fact that they restrict our behaviours and choices. Responses - chosen non-habitual behaviours - can, by contrast, feel distinctly unfamiliar and unnatural.

However, there are ways of familiarising ourselves with the unfamiliar. We can practice the pause by radiating our attention through postural and spatial landmarks during all sorts of low risk, seemingly unimportant, in-between moments of daily life - waiting at a bus stop, in line at the supermarket, at red lights, etc. By coming to balance and stillness momentarily we bring ourselves to a 'choice point' where we can consider not only what our next steps may be but what the quality of our next steps might be.

Practising pausing, stillness and coming to a choice point in this way strengthens our abilities to react appropriately when the pressure is on. Pausing helps you to stay in touch with your reasoning, i.e. the ability to think on your feet during a presentation and to negotiate a constructive path through whatever challenges life happens to be presenting you with.

Practical exercise - The Sonnet Stepping Stone

- Take three phrases from the beginning of a presentation. Let each the phrases be, very approximately, ten syllables in length.
- Take three phrases from the middle of presentation - approximately ten syllables in length
- Three closing phrases from – each approximately ten syllables
- Three phrases of 'next steps'
- Remember a phrase can simply be a part of a complete sentence.

You now have a total of twelve phrases that span the totality of your presentation. Practise them repeatedly with appropriate pausing and centring.

Having connected the main sections of your presentation in this way go on to do the same thing with each of the component sections –

- Three phrases from the beginning of the beginning section.
- Three phrases from the middle of the beginning section.
- Three phrases from the end of the beginning section.

Practise them repeatedly with appropriate pausing and centring.

Do the same for the middle, ending and next step sections.

- Chapter Thirteen -

A WORD ABOUT BREATHING

'"Yes, they are elves," Legolas said. "and they say that you breathe so loud they could shoot you in the dark." Sam hastily covered his mouth.'
J.R.R. Tolkien

TAKE A DEEP BREATH?

Singer and songwriter, Jo Maultby, is famous for being able to hold a note for more than forty seconds and at considerable volume!

Audiences find this impressive. What makes it even more impressive is that Jo is a diminutive five foot in height and has a correspondingly small ribcage. Jo maintains that she can sing these long, loud notes even if she starts with a small amount of air in her lungs.

I also know a folk club singer who sings at operatic volume on one functioning lung. My sister sings and talks effectively with one and a half lungs. Volume of sound is not ultimately dependent on volume of air. Sometimes if you take too deep a breath the air will fly away that much quicker and leave you gasping for breath.

Still it has to be said that efficient and economical breathing can do much to enhance comfort, confidence and expressiveness. By using the postural, emotional and spatial landmarks we've explored in this book you will do much to enhance the efficiency of your breathing and of your speaking voice. How you use your spine in relation to breathing and voice is a critical factor.

In addition to the following chapter, take some time to review the material in Chapter 6 about head balance.

Compressive forces

The postural tendency to contract, shortening and narrowing, the torso influences breathing significantly. The breathing mechanism is thus surrounded by converging forces which hem in and impinge on its natural rhythms of expansion and contraction.

The muscles that connect the top vertebra of the spine to the base of the skull shorten through over-contraction or collapse, and pull the head down onto the spine.

The resulting pressures travel down the spine and over-compress the discs (inter-vertebral cartilages) that lie between each vertebra.

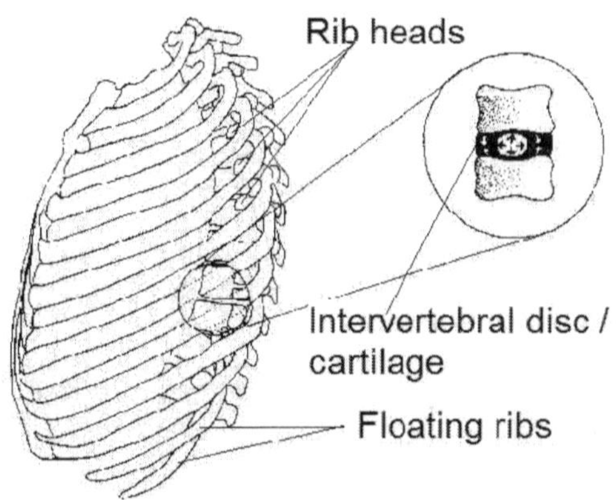

Ribs and Cartilages

The ribs radiate out from the spine at the back, with the top ten pairs attaching either directly or indirectly to the breastbone in front. The bottom two pairs of ribs are known as the floating ribs because they have no connection to the breastbone in front. At the point of attachment into the spine, the head of the rib spans the level of the inter-vertebral disc, touching both the vertebrae above it and the vertebrae below.

When the head is pulled down onto the spine, it compresses the vertebrae, discs and the head of the rib where it joins the spine. All of these factors contribute to restricting the efficient movement of the ribs and the breathing mechanism as a whole.

When someone breathes heavily through emotion or physical effort, it is usually accompanied by alternating postural rigidity and slump - a heaving upwards of the breastbone (front of the chest) on inspiration (in-breath) and a downward slumping of the breastbone on the out-breath. The head will mirror this movement by bobbing up and down to a greater or lesser degree. This elevation and depression of the breastbone is frequently present in 'normal' breathing

Expansive directions and managing the out-breath

It's helpful to think of maintaining a firm but unfixed position of the upper chest on the expiration - the out-breath. How can you help this to happen? This would be a good time to review the material in Chapter 4, starting with 'Posture, Impact and confidence' up to 'Emotion, breathing and your voice'.

Rather than sagging or slumping on the out-breath it really helps, paradoxically, to expand both spatial and postural awareness on the out-breath...

- Think of your feet on the ground...
- your head poised and balancing on top of your spine...
- your shoulders and peripheral vision widening.
-

Think of these landmarks while simply observing your out-breath or whilst whispering, vocalising or singing an 'ah' sound. Allow the in-breath to return as silently as possible.

This approach encourages your spine to lengthen and will facilitate lateral breathing by allowing the ribs tend to naturally move in a 'bucket handle action'. The ribs will move 'medially' - down and in towards the mid-line of the body during expiration, i.e. the out-breath. The ribs will move 'laterally' up and away from the spine during inspiration, i.e. the in-breath.

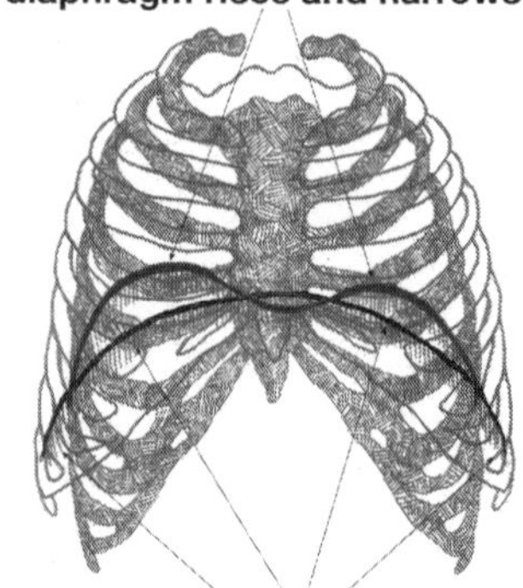

The bucket handle action of ribs during breathing –
Shaded ribcage representing the out-breath.
Un-shaded ribcage representing the in-breath.

The Diaphragm

Much is said about the diaphragm in vocal circles, yet my own informal surveys strongly suggest that more than 95% of professional voice users have a hazy or downright inaccurate idea of where it is located, its size and how it actually works. Perhaps this is not surprising - it's difficult to find a really clear drawing of the diaphragm because its dome like shape is obscured by the ribcage to which it attaches. It's an excellent idea to clarify where the diaphragm is actually located.

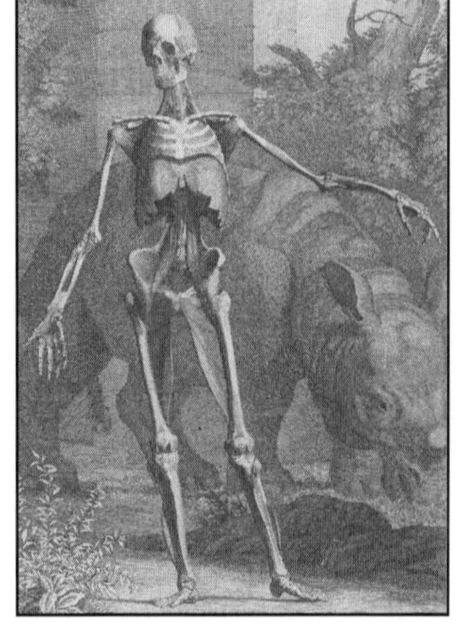

This illustration of a skeleton (with classical ruins and grazing Rhino!) by Albinus, 16th century professor of anatomy, represents one of the few clear and accurate pictures of the diaphragm available.

The diaphragm is a large dome-like muscle that divides the upper and lower torso. It attaches to the breastbone at the front, the cartilages of the ribs as they sweep down from the breastbone, the two lower 'floating' ribs and, finally, to the spine at the back.

The diaphragm is intimately linked with the psoas muscles. The psoas muscles span from the lower spine to the top of the thigh bones. They cross the pubis en route.

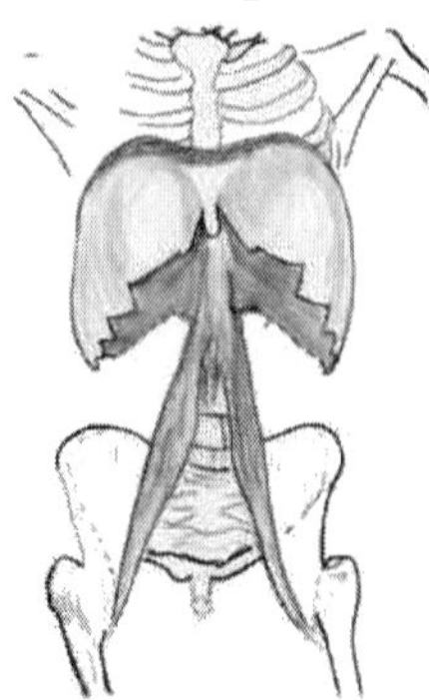

The dome of the diaphragm looks rather the body of a jelly fish. The psoas muscles look the tendrils of the jelly fish. How you plant your feet on the ground and how you use your legs has a direct effect on how you breathe.

Find, approximately, where the circumference of the diaphragm attaches to your ribs:
Use your fingers to trace from your breastbone down and out along the 'costal arch', the arch of your ribs, as they sweep back towards their connection with your spine.

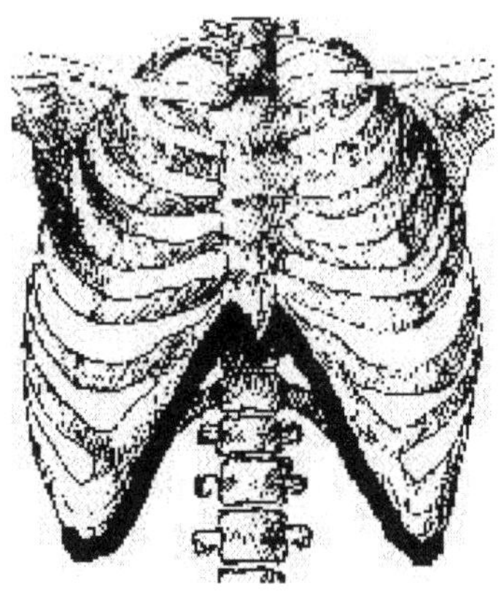

The area shaded in bold is the costal arch

You may find that you are able to feel the two lowest floating ribs that attach to the spine but have no direct connection to the breastbone. Finally, point from your navel to the corresponding area of your spine. This area of your spine is where the diaphragm anchors into your spine.

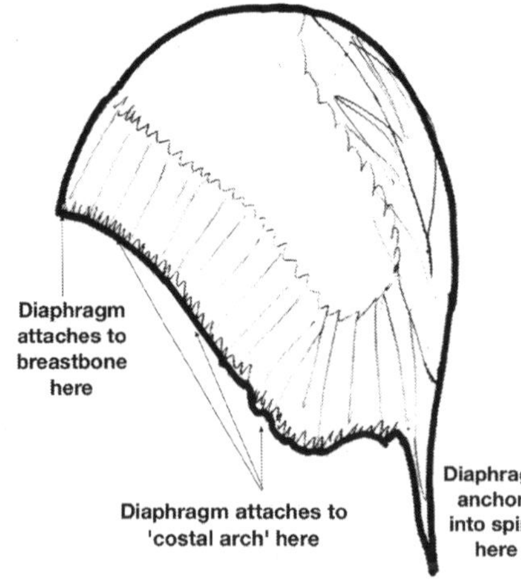

The action of the diaphragm cannot truly be considered independently of the action of the ribs. During the in-breath, the diaphragm drops lower, flatter and wider as the ribs simultaneously swing up and outwards. During the out-breath, the diaphragm rises higher, becoming more domed and narrower as the ribs drop down and in.

Practical exercise - Breathing in the semi-supine position
When you are in the semi-supine position observe how the contact and pressure of your lower back on the floor changes as you breath – increasing as you breath in and decreasing as you breath out.
Using your navel as a landmark you can slide your fingertips slightly under the corresponding part of your lower back to help you sense this.
You may also notice your sides widening as you breathe in and narrowing as you breathe out.
Although the breathing movements may be quite low in your torso they can also be gentle and minimal – there is no need for particularly deep breathing when you are lying down quietly and peacefully.

Practical exercise - Breathing in the prone position

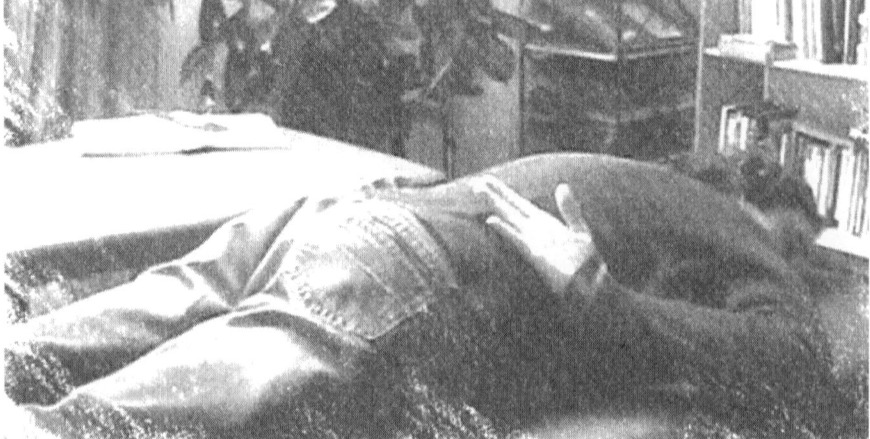

From the semi-supine position roll yourself gently over onto your front. Turn your head to one side, resting your cheek on the floor. Place the backs of your hands on the sides of your lower back. Feel your sides widening as you breathe in and narrowing as you breathe out. Be aware also of the rising of your lower back as you breathe in and falling as you breathe out.
Now transfer that awareness of breathing in the back and in the sides, to the upright positions of standing and sitting.
Place your hands gently along each side of your ribs. Radiate your attention through your postural, spatial and emotional landmarks. Simply be aware of the movement of your ribs, however large or small that might be. Place the backs of your hands on your lower back and feel the breathing movements there.

Try it in the sitting position – think of balancing delicately on the sitting bones as you do.

Summary

- Take care of the out-breath and the in-breath will take care of itself.
- Volume of air doesn't equate to volume of sound or length of sound.
- Expand to breathe out.
- Breathe in quietly.

Note: You may be surprised to hear that a comprehensive moving model of the breathing system including diaphragm doesn't yet exist. Jessica Wolf, Alexander teacher, has joined forces with animator Marty Havran to create the first three-dimensional animation that exhibits all the muscles, bones and organs of breathing. (See References)

- Chapter Fourteen -

WILLING IT AND LOVING IT

'What's money? A man is a success if he gets up in the morning and goes to bed at night and in between does what he wants to do.'
Bob Dylan

'If you have built castles in the air, your work need not be lost; that is where they should be. Now put the foundations under them.'
Henry David Thoreau

CLOUD-WATCHING

Do you remember cloud-watching as a child? Remember the familiar and fantastic patterns that you saw there?
"There's a ship!"
"Where?"
"That group of clouds over there!"
"I still don't see a ship."
"No, no. Not that group of clouds. That group of clouds there..."
"Oh yes. Now I see it. There's the bow and there's the stern..."
"And a huge funnel."
"And look, those little feathery clouds could be dolphins swimming beside the ship."
"Mmm... only if you screw your eyes up a little bit."
"And look, over there, to the left.."
"A huge lighthouse!"
"Woahoo!"
Some people turn this ability to see patterns into an interesting skill, whether crystal ball gazing or stock market speculation. Whatever your skill, the key question is "How can I increasingly make real more of my deepest desires, wishes and outcomes in life — personally and professionally?"

The big picture

All too often, people wait for fate or external circumstances to deal them an ace hand. Success is less a question of guessing what the future has in store for you and much more about having a hand - both hands - in creating your future.
For success as a presenter, turn to that most honest form of crystal ball - a trusted friend or colleague who listens quietly most of the time but will occasionally and yet persistently ask the probing questions that speak to the heart of the matter. Their feedback will allow you to stand back from the blinkered pursuit of goals, to survey the wider external and internal territory that is laid out before you and adjust your course accordingly
When you are creating your own future, you are ultimately dealing with something far more objective - your own subjective desires and wishes. The key question is:
What gets you, happily and willingly, up and out of your bed in the morning?

... and what makes the process of getting out of bed a struggle and a strain?

What gives you that 'I want to' feeling and what gives you that 'I have to' feeling?

You now know a lot of the techniques, beliefs and strategies for getting this to happen in presentations. Could they be applied to getting the 'want to' feeling to happen in more of your life?

On a very basic level, if you think of the professional options that are open to you, which ones give you that 'I want to' feeling? Of course, there may be many things that you 'have to' do and many skills that you 'must' acquire to make that happen.

Many people toss a coin when considering possible future alternatives. The beauty of this simple technique is that you will often find that you will be really disappointed with how the coin falls - and this in itself helps to clarify your true feelings about the course of action you truly want to take.

Planning your life

We don't all live to work. Many people work to live and their true creative identities may be more grounded in their unpaid but highly rewarding social activities. Nonetheless, the same questions hold true. What specific steps will help to bring about a much closer fit between you, the person and you, the role that you represent?

As well as considering what you want to be doing and how you are going to get sufficient skills to fulfil the role, you should consider the time scale involved. How long will it take you to get there? Six months? One year? More?

It is worth considering that a small change in one area can make all the difference to the all-round feeling of your professional and personal life.

Remember the Zen saying:

Climb the mountain one small step at a time... and when you reach the top, keep on climbing.

Resources

Society of Teachers of the Alexander Technique (STAT) – Alexander Technique teachers can help you with posture, breathing, movement and controlling stage nerves. http://www.stat.org.uk/ Tel. 0207 482 5135
Mail office@stat.org.uk

Toastmasters International - an organisation with 13,500 clubs in 116 countries that helps people to develop their public speaking and communication skills. Based around regular meetings - be an observer and, in your own time, start to deliver presentations in a supportive atmosphere with constructive feedback. Toastmasters is a low fee, not-for-profit organisation. http://www.toastmasters.org/

Cheryl Ann Winter - a valued contributor to this book. Cheryl offers both individual and group coaching. http://www.cawskills.com/

Alexander Technique in Ireland –Richard Brennan for courses, individual coaching and professional training. http://www.alexander.ie/
NLP – For information and resources on NLP
NLP conferences in the UK http://www.nlpconference.co.uk/
ANLP the Association for NLP professionals http://www.anlp.org/
Professional Guild of NLP - http://www.professionalguildofnlp.com/

Tony Buzan - inventor of Mind Mapping! http://www.thinkbuzan.com/intl/

Michael Gelb – Alexander Technique teacher and author of many personal development books. Michael introduced me Mind Mapping when we were fellow Alexander students. http://michaelgelb.com/

Coaching and Courses with Alan Mars

Individual Coaching

Skype Coaching – a surprisingly immediate and effective experience!

Corporate Coaching

Face to face
Face to face via Skype
Group training sessions
Train the trainer

Webinars

Public Workshops

Keep in touch with Alan's workshop and coaching schedule by visiting his website www.thetechnique.co.uk/

Email – alan.mars@yahoo.co.uk

Phone – 07930 323 057

Alan Mars

For the past 30 years Alan Mars has coached delegates from many leading public and private businesses and organisations. These include: Abbey National, Adobe, BMW, BNFL, Boots, Brighton and Hove Council, BT, Central Bank of Malta, Church of England, Collins, Consumers Association, EDF Energy, General Electric, Lloyds of London, Royal Pharmaceutical Society, Sainsbury's and many others.

He has taught Alexander Technique and voice-work at many top performing arts schools, including the Arts Educational Drama School, the Guildhall School of Music and Drama and the Royal College of Music.

His first book, 'Presenter – Be Your Best… and Beyond' *(Hodder Arnold, 2003)*, is a guide to motivating teams and individuals to improving their key skills in presenting. Further books in the 'Confidence Tricks' series are planned for release 2013-2015.

He has taken the best techniques from the world of the performing arts, Alexander Technique and NLP and adapted them for use in business and commercial settings.

Alan runs a busy private coaching practice Brighton & Hove and offers courses and personal coaching across the UK. Alan is also a professional musician, singer and a black belt Aikido teacher.

For more information visit **www.thetechnique.co.uk**
or contact **alan.mars@yahoo.co.uk**

Use these pages to make reminders, prompts and notes for your own personal reference.

Notes:

Printed in Great Britain
by Amazon.co.uk, Ltd.,
Marston Gate.